GET 2020 VISION

I0091348

AWESOME COACHING

Mental Wellness Edition

IMPACT YOUR LIFE WITH
COMPASSION, PATIENCE & CURIOSITY

DAVE ROGERS

WITH TRACEY REGAN

ISBN 978-0-6487192-4-3

_____

To Mother and Father
for being shining lights
of the human experiment.

Appreciate you individually.
Thank you for sharing the life journey
and love you both immensely.

_____

CONTENTS

THE COMPANY DAVE KEEPS!

"I have known Dave for over 15 years and one thing always stands out about him is consistent result-delivering interventions. He understands the underlying psychological and emotional triggers that either boost or hamper performance and he tackles them head on to create long lasting results......always."
      – Billy Selekane CSP , SASHoF, SAEHoF, EXPY - Founder and President : Billy Selekane International , South Africa

"The depth of one's character is illuminated through their scope of service and perseverance in making the universe a little better one day at a time. Dave is a beacon of contribution through his coaching, teaching and open-heartedness. Since meeting him in 2008 he continues to walk the talk."
      – Deb Maybury, Author, Speaker & Psychotherapist. Toronto, Canada

"When you listen to Dave speak or read what he has written, you will reflect and learn a lot more about yourself. Dave's knowledge, ability to communicate and passion are evident in everything he does. AWESOME COACHING will definitely take you to the next level of your personal journey."
      – Ian Botnick, Principal, Toronto District School Board

"Dave is not the coach, he makes me feel like I am the coach in our relationship. He affirms my views and is ever curious about my thoughts. In this flipped-coaching relationship I've had with him over the years, his humour and honesty floats me, as I deal with constant deaths."
      – LK Tan, Hospice nurse, Singapore

"David has a unique way of engaging people and enriching their lives by asking deep questions that bring clarity to past issues and current challenges that may be holding a person back."
      – Todd Hutchison, Global CEO, Peopleistic, Australia

"After first meeting Dave in 2007 and enjoying his energy, enthusiasm and curiosity about others, I've very much benefited personally and professionally from our ongoing association. Able to sit quietly with others and simply hold a safe space to express themselves while sharing his vast knowledge so freely, working closely with Dave is a treasured experience.

Dave has prompted me to ask better questions and to be curious about other possibilities. When supporting those experiencing mental health challenges, grief or other emotional drains, Dave uses the resources shown in this book, and many other skills and techniques, to create a life shift. Once others have been in a coaching session with Dave, they'll never be the same and that'll be a good thing! Like me, they'll be grateful for the awesomeness Dave brings."

– Gillian Robinson, Registered Nurse, Aged Care Software Designer and Consultant / Author, New Zealand.

"Dave Rogers is a highly inspirational, world-class success coach, speaker and author. For over 20 years, I have watched him transform people through the sharing of his wisdom, love and compassion. He thrives on helping people achieve personal breakthroughs even in the most challenging times. This book will be extremely beneficial for those who are facing challenges in life or are in a caregiving role. Thumbs up!"

– Wendy Kwek, WK Events, Singapore

"Dave is one of the few rare people we meet in life who truly listens, honestly communicates and shares wisdom and knowledge freely from a heart-centred space. He is an AWESOME coach, and an authentic and compassionate person who has encouraged me, inspired me and challenged me to look at life differently, considering alternative perspectives and possibilities. Working with Dave has significantly changed my life, and as you work through this book, you too may experience a shift that could impact your life in unexpected ways."

– Tracey Regan, Author / business owner, Australia

"I was taught to serve with compassion, respect, humility and love. Dave reminds me of this during our chats and informal debriefs after my missions. He has the ability to show me the 'other side of the coin' and always does this with love and humility."
- Gurudev Singh, Nurse, New Zealand Red Cross & Florence Nightingale Medal recipient

"Dave Rogers is a master coach who puts his heart into coaching and unleashing human potential. He lives by the words he shares in this book, which is perhaps the greatest testimony to their power."
– Lisa McCarthy, Founder and Director Wealth Dynamics International Ltd, New Zealand

"Dave Rogers is one of the foremost results-driven coaches of the 21st century. You will have much to gain from his words of wisdom. His book will be an all time classic for both serious coaches and forward-looking clients. Give a copy to your friends if you treasure friendships and aim to transform lives for a better tomorrow."
– Patrick Liew, Director-SkyQuestCom, Singapore

"It takes genius to make a complex subject simple to understand without losing effectiveness. As someone who has benefited greatly from Dave's coaching and now have the pleasure of reviewing his new book, I can say that his new book, like his coaching is simple but powerful! In other words a work of genius which I highly recommend."
– Jacob Ho, Vice Chairman Green Harmony Co., Bangkok, THAILAND

"Dave Rogers is an Awesome coach. He uses the word "awesome" liberally, seeing people as awesome and making me feel awesome. Yet his approach to coaching is the essence of simplicity. Simplicity comes when there is clarity, which is what Dave seeks. He is the master of asking questions - the right questions. Dave is the antithesis of the overbearing, fire-spitting sports coach. He is actually quite endearing. I find it easy to open up to him because he really seeks to serve and communicates so respectfully."
– Dr James Chia, Financial Planner, Leadership Coach

FOREWORD
BY RON KAUFMAN

Dave Rogers is committed to results. He is committed to making an awesome and positive impact. He is committed to your better life. Dave is willing to listen, but your story will not stop him. He will let you share your reasons, but your reasoning will not distract him.

Dave Rogers is a man on a mission: helping you become the best that you can be.

So he will dig in. He will go after you. He will listen better, probe deeper, and attack you with more passion – and compassion – than you can imagine for yourself. Dave Rogers loves his work as much as he loves his life, as much as he loves you. And he wants you to become your very best.

That's why you contacted him, right? That's why you picked up this book. You want the kind of improvement in your life (and the lives of those around you) that makes others say "Wow! What happened to you?" You want to say to yourself "Wow! Why did I wait so long?"

Perhaps you are tired of the little stories that protect your little life. Or you want to help others discover a bigger world they can create and share with those around them. If so, you have come to the right place.

If you are ready for an awesome change in the way you have been living, then you are reading the right book. If you are ready to make an awesome impact as a coach in the lives of others, then you have the right coach in your hands to show you how.

WELCOME TO THE INCREDIBLE WORLD OF THE AWESOME COACH, DAVE ROGERS. I AM SURE YOU WILL ENJOY THE RIDE.

~ RON KAUFMAN Bestselling Author, "Up Your Service"

"Becoming a leader is synonymous with becoming yourself.

It is precisely that simple and is also that difficult."

~ Warren Bennis

It has been fifteen years since Awesome Coaching was first printed in Singapore and I am excited to invite you to the Get 2020 Vision & Mental Wellness Special Edition

INTRODUCTION

"There is always a light within us that is free from all sorrow and grief, no matter how much we may be experiencing suffering."
~ Patanjali

With a focus on Mental Wellness, the new opening chapters in this special edition are on dealing with Depression, Suicide and Men's Mental Health, Loneliness and Corporate Post Traumatic Stress Disorder, Death & Grief, as well as a comprehensive chapter on Discovering Your True North Purpose, and mapping out your bespoke GPS calibration system.

With the unprecedented global lockdown seen in early 2020 due to the COVID-19 virus, these chapters are more relevant today than ever before. We must all be aware of our Mental Wellness, as well as ensuring to observe the Mental Wellness of our family, our friends, and our colleagues.

In compiling the first edition of Awesome Coaching, most of the stories and experiences were from the "gestalt" (first-hand experience) perspective, and as with this version, contained practical approaches to infuse awesome impact coaching into the workplace.

These experiences have come from my seventeen years working in the highly-stressed world of the financial markets as a corporate risk manager in Japan, five years as a fixed income bond trader in Hong Kong, and transitioning Corporate Financier. Others are from my life as a freshly minted, optimistic, social entrepreneur, international facilitator and award-winning business coach based out of Singapore.

In the first edition of Awesome Coaching, we presented strategies for bringing coaching into the workplace. We focused on simple, effective, and straightforward techniques to improve productivity, raise morale and increase employee satisfaction both in and outside of the office.

In this special 2020 Get Vision and Mental Wellness Edition, we update the content to infuse wellbeing, resilience and mental wellness into our lives, as well as address the top four or five relevant issues facing employees, leaders and entrepreneurs in 2020.

As you read this Get 2020 Vision Edition of Awesome Coaching, I invite you to reflect, breathe, ponder and write your short answers, keywords or learnings, as an experiential approach to engage in the process of accelerated learning.

Fifteen years since the launch of Awesome Coaching, my editor for this project asked me "What are some of the biggest challenges facing people today?" I took a deep breath, reached for my dear friend Google and searched for the most stressful life events that may trigger depression. The list appeared and I invite you to check off those which apply to you.

10 COMMON DEPRESSION TRIGGERS

- **Do you feel overwhelmed or stressed?**
- **Have you experienced a significant health condition or situation?**
- **Do you know what it feels like to lose your job, career or business?**
- **Are you financially stressed or pressured?**
- **Have you experienced relationship challenges?**
- **Do you have a weight problem?**
- **Are you struggling with difficult life transitions?**
- **Do you have alcohol or other substance problems?**
- **Do you have a poor diet?**
- **Are your suffering from poor sleep habits?**

According to our research, conducted in more than 43 countries and supplemented with coaching people who have experienced all of the aforementioned stressful life events, if you have checked off five or more from the list above, it is likely that you may be suffering from depression.

As I inhale deeply, smile, breathe and answer the questions, I notice that I have experienced each one of the stressful events listed. I have checked off every question!

- **Stressed out in 1987 to a point where I contemplated suicide.**
- **Heart surgery in 2006 to repair a blockage in my descending artery.**
- **Made redundant from my ex-pat finance job in Singapore December 17, 2000**
- **Marital separation in 2019 and business separation in 2008 and 2019**
- **Weight ballooned to 200++ pounds in 1987 and 2018**
- **Alcoholism and sexual addition in 1987**
- **Poor diet in 1987**
- **Poor sleep habits in 2019**

This has resulted in my discovery of several approaches, strategies and perspectives that may assist you in your own professional and personal journey.

In this book, I will share insights and distinctions that led me to some winning (and not-so winning) strategies.

Since returning to Canada in 2019 after a 33-year journey working primarily in Tokyo, Hong Kong and Singapore, and in preparing for this 2020 Get Vision Edition, I was surprised by the number of people who have approached me with a list of personal and professional problems such as confusion, lack of direction, sense of overwhelm or even boredom.

With further study, I discovered that mental illness has become an epidemic in North America. Overwhelm transitions into depression, anxiety, and panic attacks, and then can shift into suicidal thoughts, bi-polar, and post-traumatic stress disorder. This has become a major health issue across the world.

After consulting numerous doctors, nurses and health care workers, as well as my editor, the Get 2020 Vision Edition of Awesome Coaching became a work in progress. Today I am pleased to have it in your hands for your review, for you to read and to experience. I hope it will engage you to apply some of your favorite coaching practices and allow yourself to adapt some fine tuning to your communication, and to educate and equip yourself with some new approaches or perspectives in nurturing and serving yourself and others.

As you know "readers are leaders" and I congratulate you on embracing this book and exploring ways that wisdom and experiences can assist you on your journey, which in turn will serve you to assist others.

Let's explore some of the numbers around mental wellness and mental illness, as a framework to explore ways that we can increase awareness, embrace challenges and equip you with some approaches that can make a difference.

"Discover yourself, otherwise, you have to depend on other people's opinions, who don't know themselves."

~ Osho

WORLDWIDE STATISTICS

*Depression is the leading cause of
disability worldwide*

In developing countries, almost 75% of people with mental disorders remain untreated, with almost 1 million people taking their lives each year.

Major Depressive Disorder

MDD affects more than 16.1 million American adults, or about 6.7% of the US population aged 18 and older in a given year and is the leading cause of disability in the US for ages 15 to 44.3. While Major Depressive Disorder can develop at any age, the average age at onset is 32.5 years old. It is more prevalent in women than in men.

Post-traumatic Stress Disorder (PTSD)

PTSD affects 7.7 million adults or 3.5% of the US population. Women are more likely to be affected than men. Rape is the most likely trigger of PTSD, 65% of men and 45.9% of women who are raped will develop the disorder. Childhood sexual abuse is a strong predictor of lifetime likelihood for developing PTSD.

The American Foundation for Suicide Prevention reported that in 2016, suicide was the 10th leading cause of death in the US, imposing a cost of $69 billion to the US annually.

Any surprises around the numbers above?

From my experience, statistics are grossly understated for mental illness and suicide, especially in Asia. From my seventeen years in the financial markets, I observed, learned, and noticed that almost any argument, statistic or hypothesis, can be justified by changing the data points, amending the criteria or asking leading questions.

As a point of reference, remember that 87% of statistics are made up

......and, yes I just made up that statistic. I am not encouraging you to doubt all statistics, but I am inviting you to be curious about the source of the statistics, the methodology of the polling data, and to be aware that you or your condition may be a statistical anomaly and might not fall into the range of statistically valid.

In a recent wellness and vitality coaching session, Joe was detailing his journey about being depressed, sad and lethargic, yet remained curious as to what foods and vitamins were best for him. Despite two rounds of testing with a doctor and numerous drugs being prescribed, Joe was not able to shake the foggy and tired feelings especially when taking the medication.

We discussed his various options;

1. Take all the medication and keep eating without any awareness;
2. Take the medicine while managing and recording what he ate and how he felt; or
3. Reduce the medicine, water fast for two days and then reset his wellness awareness meter by journaling and recording all foods, vitamins, exercise, and hydration that he explored.

Joe chose option three, and after a week he noticed a remarkable improvement, reduced fogginess, and felt rejuvenated, empowered and aware of changes in his eating. The dramatic leap in wellness occurred when he acknowledged that his body was like a finely tuned sports car (he loves cars), and that he was going to place his dietary awareness as one of the top priorities in his life.

He realized that his old approach was like feeding a supercharged sports car with regular gasoline and he became aware that he was going to recommit to his wellness, his nutrition, and his vitality.

After 91 days, Joe, who is nearly 57 years of age, goes to the gym 4-5 days a week, juices regularly, knows his body's reaction to different foods and vitamins intimately and is feeling like a fit, firm and friendly thirty-year-old.

Joe's winning strategy demonstrated the RESEARCH approach :

Results   **E**ducate   **S**ample
Experiment   **A**wareness
Record Data
Curiosity
Honest Learning Cycles

The inspiration to encourage people to Get 2020 Vision Mental Wellness Special Edition has many backstories....or story behind the story, or story behind the story behind the story!

For the past decade, I have utilized the metaphor of the story behind the story to provide myself and my clients with an easy to follow approach to appreciate alternative perspectives, rather than getting stuck in the rigid 'right or wrong' perspective that is so prevalent in the standard education systems around the world.

I feel blessed to share the new chapters, Depression Saved My Life, Suicide & Men's Mental Health, Death and the Grief Model, and Loneliness and Corporate Post Traumatic Stress Disorder. For this Special Edition, I am thankful to the health practitioners that added their experiences, expertise and perspectives to the information shared, to the associates who agreed to share their personal stories and the creative team who made this book a reality.

I'm also excited to share the True North Purpose Finder and Personalized GPS Calibration Process, and hope to share this in an upcoming Masterclass online and face to face.

Many thanks and kind blessings to my editing team, designers, associates, friends and family in encouraging me to deliver this special Mental Wellness edition of Awesome Coaching and may 2020 prove to offer unexpected opportunities and loving moments that can be cherished. I encourage you to live in the moment and not with the fear of what may be!

Respect and blessings of love and light
Dave Rogers

*Depression isn't something
anyone should have to
struggle with on their own*

DEPRESSION

I feel like statistics are understating the extent of depression in society, yet according to the Mental Health Commission of Canada, 11% of men and 16% of women in Canada will experience major depression at some time in their lives.

In the USA, according to the Anxiety and Depression Association of America (ADAA), nearly 15 million people suffer from depression, and for 22% of these people it is persistent depression, meaning it's a depressive episode that lasts for longer than two years and doesn't go away on its own, or the sufferer has frequent depressive episodes that continue to reoccur.

Depression can affect our quality of life, hinder relationships, lead to lost time from work or school and contribute to other chronic diseases such as diabetes and heart disease. Sometimes it can lead to suicide. Fortunately, for most people, depression can be treated effectively.

Everyone's journey has ups and downs, periods of unhappiness, sadness, grief, boredom, and depression in their lives. Most people become temporarily 'down' when things don't seem to be going well, and this is viewed as a normal stream of life.

Job dissatisfaction, the loss of a loved one or a breakdown in a relationship can trigger a down-cycle in your emotions, yet staying depressed for extended periods could be an indicator of major depression.

Major depression is a clinical term used by psychiatrists to define a period of time that lasts more than two months, in which a person feels worthless and helpless.

Depression can affect
the way you think and behave
and can also have
physical effects as well

Here are some signs to be aware of when considering the possibility of depression:

- **Feeling lost, sad, hopeless, or generally unhappy**
- **Changes in sleeping habits ranging from difficulties falling asleep to insomnia to spending most of your time in bed or being too lethargic to move or too unmotivated to get out of bed**
- **Lack of energy that makes even simple everyday tasks seem difficult or too hard**
- **Detachment from life and the people around you**
- **Crying for no apparent reason**
- **Not being able to concentrate or make decisions**
- **Easily agitated, anxious and restless**
- **Lack of joy from activities you previously enjoyed (dancing, singing, walking or hobbies, etc)**
- **Slowed thinking or difficulty paying attention**
- **Feeling worthless or not good enough (often in conjunction with overthinking past mistakes or failures)**
- **Feeling guilty about things that aren't your fault or are out of your control**
- **Frequent or recurrent thoughts of death or suicide**
- **Physical issues, such as headaches, stomach ache or muscle pain**

**Mayo Clinic Staff, n.d

TRIGGERS OF DEPRESSION

Many factors contribute to the onset of depression. I have experienced that some people may be genetically disposed to depression and their risk may be elevated when triggered by external factors.

External factors that can trigger depression are

- **Major illness or death of a family member, friend or even a celebrity**
- **Challenges in personal relationships or at work**
- **Bullying or sexual abuse**
- **Addictions**
- **In Canada, many people suffer from Seasonal Affective Disorder (SAD) which affects people from late January through to March when there is less natural light**
- **Due to hormonal changes, women may experience postpartum depression after giving birth or depression around menopause**
- **Sense of failure, low self-esteem or financial difficulties**

Depression is an illness that can be treated!

RECOVERY FROM DEPRESSION

In coaching clients with mood disorders, overwhelm or depression, I have found communication, curiosity, and nurturing a step-by-step approach, is essential to embracing the symptoms of the illness. Mapping out a program of resourcefulness, harmony and peace is essential for healing.

The first step in the recovery process is the awareness that depression is an illness and not a sign of weakness, shame or embarrassment.

Exploring the symptoms and seeking greater knowledge with empathy, is paramount in dealing with depression. Willingness to experiment with a wider range of healing modalities can open the door to looking at depression in a favorable manner and is a major step forward in accepting depression as a natural occurrence in our lives.

Knowing that you are not alone, and that caring approaches and innovative experiments can be embraced, allows you to find an approach that works best for you.

"One is never afraid of the unknown;
one is afraid of the unknown
coming to an end."
~ Jiddu Krishnamurti

Case Study From Japan - Developing the Vitality Plan

In working with a twenty-two-year-old creative in Japan, we distilled her winning strategy for feeling depressed and found :

1. Her self-talk was very negative. She repeated that she was a loser, had no friends, and that no one liked her.
2. She would eat chocolate, ice cream, chips, and drink soda to a point of throwing up or sleeping.
3. She would go to bed, lie down, and watch television or binge on YouTube.
4. Her mantra was, "I am depressed. I am so depressed and so alone. Nobody understands me."
5. Sometimes she would cry, and sometimes she found she had no more tears to cry.

I congratulated her and sincerely gave her an "A" on designing a terrific strategy for feeling depressed. She was not aware that her approach would trigger her hormonally, emotionally and physically, and that would ultimately get her body and mind to shut down.

The result was lethargy; a body shut down with a desire to sleep to stop the pain.

On the flip side, I asked her what she likes to do or loves to do. Her first response was, "I don't know." This is a natural answer to the question, as many school systems around the world these days do not teach young people to answer questions. There is little discussion or debate to deal with varying opinions, views or perspectives.

I rephrased the question to, "When you are feeling energetic, vibrant, or happy, what are two or three things that you enjoy doing?"

I then added, "Look up to the right, take a deep breath and either open or close your eyes." A little smile came to her face, she inhaled as she closed her eyes, and tilted her head upwards to the right.

Out spurted a part of Emiko's winning approach to feeling resourceful or energized. She noted:

I like to draw or sketch   I like to walk in nature
I like working out with full force   I like reading

I then asked her, "If you designed a vitality plan, what would be two or three things that you would have in your personalized plan?"

She took a deep breath, closed her eyes, and looked upward to the right.
"I'd hydrate with water, ensuring at least 6-8 glasses of water a day. I'd stretch at least twice a day, preferably once when I woke up and once before I went to bed. I'd have at least 2-3 runs or bike or swim sessions a week. I'd eat healthy, water-rich, green fresh vegetables, less junk food, and eat for vitality."

My third question was, "What would you change or reduce in your Personalized Resourcefulness - Depression Management System?"

Once again, she smiled, closed her eyes and looked upwards to the right and shared:

"I'd cut the sugary drinks, chips and ice cream out of my vitality plan, though maybe make it once a month as a celebration on hitting targets or goals. I'd start talking more nicely to myself. I would manage my words and I would start mantras such as, 'I am love, I am forgiveness, I am kindness,' and I'd allow myself allocated depression time in my bed for pre-agreed time frames, like 17 minutes to lay on my bed and feel depressed or 13 minutes to cry and release or 9 minutes to be a lazy lump on a log."

I smiled and congratulated Emiko on designing a wonderful approach to dealing with depression. I asked her what she would like to call her new plan.

She liked the Vitality Plan and agreed that she would like to experiment with it for the next 21 days and see what happened with her vitality and her ability to deal with depression, as well as to see what measurable results might emerge from the experiment.

We brought together her Vitality Plan and this is what it looked like:

Lighten up - Daily Activities
- I like to draw or sketch
- I like to walk in nature
- I like reading
- I like working out with full force

Energy Up - Consume For Vitality
- I will hydrate with water, ensuring at least 6-8 glasses a day
- I will stretch at least twice a day, preferably once when I wake up and once before bed
- I will have at least 2-3 runs or bike or swim sessions a week
- I will eat healthy, water-rich, green fresh vegetables, eat less junk food, and eat for vitality

Let Go - Positive Alignment
- I'll cut out the sugary drinks, chips and ice cream from my vitality plan, though maybe make it a treat once a month as a celebration on hitting targets or goals
- I'll start talking nicer to myself. I'll manage my words and start mantras such as, "I am love, I am forgiveness, I am kindness."
- I'll allow myself allocated depression time in my bed for pre-agreed time frames, like 17 minutes to lay on my bed and feel depressed, or 13 minutes to cry and release, or 9 minutes to be a lazy lump on a log

RESOURCEFULNESS AND DEPRESSION

One thing I have noticed in my years of dealing with depression and in assisting clients and friends in dealing with their depression, is that each individual is unique, requiring a different approach to recovery.

The most common and successful treatment is coaching, hypnotherapy, and psychological counseling combined with anti-depressant medication.

If you, or someone close to you, suffers from depression, these awareness points may be of support or assistance.

- Avoid blaming and shaming, as no individual or family member should feel responsible for depression. Depression is an illness that often comes with complex backstories, unknown triggers and unique remedies. Blaming someone for their depression or telling them to "pull themselves together" doesn't help, and may further isolate the individual.

- Be curious and explore as a compassionate seeker. Talk to your family doctor, certified coach or a mental health professional about depression. Research, experiment and join your family member or friend on the journey, as together your might accelerate the collective learning and approaches to serve. For more details check out 'Curiosity' (Page 141).

- Nurture good listening and try to get the person who is depressed to explore their emotions (energy in motion), feelings and thoughts. Invite them to express and let them know that it's OK to talk about these things. Avoid prescribing remedies or contradicting, and practice attentive listening. Review 'Listening' for some tips (Page 101).

- Collective Community Support - invite and involve other friends and family members, if the person with depression agrees. Invite compassionate, experienced and caring support. Support from family, friends, co-workers and self-help groups can make a big difference in how well and how quickly the person with depression recovers.

One approach that I have discovered and embraced to engage depression and loneliness, as well as happiness and joy and a connection to nature, is writing poetry. Inspired by my dear friend and male Mental Health advocate, Harley Springer in Perth, Australia, we explored poetry as a way to harness, articulate and direct emotions, or energy in motion, onto paper, or our handheld devices, in order to get our mindset into a modality of flow, glow and go go go. One of the poems I wrote in 2019, as a prescriptive healing process that invites feedback experimentation, follows.

A Healing Experience

Breathe
Breathe
Breathe

Allow a sniffle and a tear
Appreciate the energy, notice the fear

Breathe in deeply, inhale and be
Exhale and notice, what do you see?

Listen closely, to the sounds you hear
Sensing each beat, far or near

Ask, what is the message for you today?
Is there healing? Sharing? Or wisdom to say?

Avoid judging the experience, criticizing yourself
Welcome, embrace, the message may deliver true wealth

Ask ways to harness, feel and release the energy
BreathWork, inhale, exhale - will bring you the Qi (read key)

Pain is an illusion that passes like clouds, if detach
Ask to understand the pain and it may release like a latch

What is the message of the trip?
Listen, listen, the wisdom may be in the blip

Breathe in curiosity and notice the shift
Pulse, vibration, the intensity of the lift

Exhale with wellness, release and let go
Notice without judgment as you reconnect with your flow

Be forgiving and kind, rather than wrong or right
Invite the compassion, the healing of the light

Through the breath, explore peace and serenity
Notice, observe, please do see

Kindly invite harmony and engage in a caring call
Rather than judging, criticizing, and knowing it all

Allow in the innocence of inquiry, humility and awe
Be truthfully naked and vulnerably raw

Be present to the newness the brain does not know
Breathe, breathe, simply breathe and gracefully let go

Breathe, Breathe, Breathe is my mantra today
Inhale, exhale with joy and peace is my new way

Namaste Namaste, is my cue
May the divine in me honor the divine in you.

Breathe, Breathe, Breathe

"Poetry heals the wounds inflicted by reason."
~ Novalis

Did you know that more than half of all suicides involve people aged 45 or older?

MENTAL HEALTH FOR MEN
IS SUICIDE THE ONLY OPTION?

Are you aware that mental illness is a leading cause of disability in Canada? Are you surprised that the economic burden of mental illness in Canada is estimated at $51 Billion per year? This includes health care costs, lost productivity, and reductions in health-related quality of life.

Here are some of the statistics about Canadian men and their mental health situation

According to the CMHA Men and Mental Health report from August 2018, around 10% of Canadian men experience significant mental health challenges in their life. My experience suggests that this number is significantly under-reported, and I believe, that 3 out of 4 men (or 75%), will suffer from debilitating mental illness at least once in their professional career.

Sunnybrook Health Science Centre in its August 2018 report, guesstimated that approximately one million men suffer from major depression each year.

Health at a Glance in the same year, reported that approximately 4000 Canadians commit suicide annually and 75% are men. Canadian indigenous men are 11 times more likely to commit suicide, and once again, my personal experience suggests that these numbers are dramatically under-reported.

The American Foundation for Suicide Prevention reported that in 2016, suicide was the 10th leading cause of death in the US, imposing a cost of $69 billion to the US annually.

Other statistics reported are:

1. Men die by suicide 3.53x more often than women.
2. White males accounted for 7 of 10 suicides in 2016.
3. A firearm is used in almost 50% of all suicides.
4. The rate of suicide is highest in middle age—white men in particular.

"Each of us has a unique part to play
in the healing of the world."
~ Maryanne Williamson

Risk Factors

The most common risk factors for suicide are:

- **Using drugs and/or alcohol to help cope with emotions, relationships, the pressure of work or other issues**
- **Social isolation or living alone**
- **Not being able to form or sustain meaningful relationships**
- **Divorce or relationship breakdown**
- **A history of physical and/or sexual abuse**
- **Imprisonment**
- **Being bullied at school, college or work**
- **Unemployment**
- **Loss of a loved one through trauma or disease**
- **Mental illness, particularly where this is related to depression and painful or debilitating illnesses or conditions**

In older men, suicide is most strongly associated with depression, physical pain and illness, living alone, and feelings of hopelessness and guilt.

Famed psychologist Carl Jung says the midlife crisis usually occurs between the ages of 35-64, and is considered a normal part of the maturing process. The phenomenon is described as a psychological crisis brought about by events that highlight a person's growing age, inevitable mortality, and possibly shortcomings of accomplishments in life.

Emotions experienced during this phase may include depression, remorse, and anxiety, or the desire to achieve youthfulness or make drastic changes to their current lifestyle.

Why are men killing themselves?

MALE GENDER ROLES - Emotional expression is still considered inappropriate in most traditional cultures and sectors of society. Men are told to be tough and powerful, and that asking for help is a sign of weakness. They are expected to find solutions on their own. Rigid or old-fashioned gender norms may make it difficult for men to reach out and ask for support when they need it.

Depression is significantly under-diagnosed in men. Men rarely disclose feelings of depression to their doctors. When they do, it is often described in terms of having problems at work or in relationships. Men also tend to describe their feelings as "stress," rather than sadness or hopelessness.

Men are less likely to seek help for emotional problems

Depression is diagnosed less frequently in men because of the tendency to deny illness, to self-monitor symptoms, and to self-treat.

Men may be more likely to self-treat symptoms of depression with alcohol and other substances. Furthermore, while suicide attempts are a cry for help, men are more likely to choose drastic and lethal methods.

EXPLORING SOLUTIONS - Open Forum Conversation

During a mastermind session, with the Afro-Caribbean Business Network I co-facilitated in Brampton at the Empower 4 x Excellence co-working space, the topic of midlife crisis emerged, and participants shared that positive and constructive behavior may be developed or launched during the midlife crisis phase of life.

Participant discussion included:

• Being better informed on mental illness, depression and suicide. By investigating, researching and having conversations about these topics, we can be part of the solution to reduce the stigma around mental illness.

• Communicating with friends and family with curiosity, patience and empathy, when you or others may be experiencing anxiety, stress and various forms of mental illness including depression, panic attacks and personality disorders.

• Some might explore inside out, with a focus on truly getting to know oneself, being curious, expressing empathy and developing self-awareness about your values, wants and desires.

• Avoiding judgment, blame and guilt, as these behaviors will likely add to the burden experienced, rather than assist with finding solutions.

• Getting professional help, joining a support group or getting involved in environments that will allow you to develop new skills, expand your awareness or understanding of mental health and mental illness, and explore steps to nurture empathy, compassion and self-care.

- Infusing your life with new words, motivational signs and inspirational phrases, and eliminating words that lead to confusion, frustration and overwhelm. We call this transformational vocabulary and participants noted that "changing your words can change your life."

- Exploring healthy and vibrant eating and wellness plans. By changing our eating, hydration, and vitality plans, we can give our body and mind new ingredients for well-being and wellness. Drink healthy clean water, eat fruits and vegetables, and exercise regularly.

- Expressing oneself through art, music or dance can lead to new businesses, new connection and new opportunities. New businesses, jobs or career possibilities can be explored.

- Retail therapy and shopping may trigger some positive changes for self- image, self-esteem and self-confidence. A midlife crisis might invite the purchase of a nice, new car or starting afresh with a vibrant new relationship.

- Developing a mental wellness plan with approximate timelines, milestones and measures that can be diarized, recorded and designed to support your journey. Allocate yourself ample time, resources and flexibility, to design a self-care program that can work well for you. Perhaps work with a buddy or accountability partner who can assist, guide and support your progress.

- Embrace self-care, self-discovery and service in your life, and invite healthy, vibrant and active learning in your environment.

The Mastermind group suggested infusing healthy thinking, inspirational reading or watching motivational videos on Youtube as a good start.

The top tips from the session were:

Les Brown - Chinese Bamboo Tree
https://www.youtube.com/watch?v=0e1LYMhgxTk

Steve Harvey - You Have To Jump
https://www.youtube.com/watch?v=-PdjNJz7B1Q

Lisa Nichols - Find Your Way Back
https://www.youtube.com/watch?v=2eJHa-sMpzg

Brene Brown - The Power of Vulnerability
https://www.youtube.com/watch?v=iCvmsMzlF7o

I would like to add another that might assist in the personalization of your wellness plan : The GPS Life Calibration System. You can view it at
https://www.youtube.com/watch?v=0np0ktoK3AQ&t=12s

The best people possess a feeling for beauty, the courage to take risks, the discipline to tell the truth, the capacity to sacrifice. Ironically, their virtues make them vulnerable; they are often wounded, sometimes destroyed.'
~Ernest Hemingway

Be realistic:
plan for a miracle!
~ Osho

Why me? Why does this always happen to me? Why God? Why did this have to happen?

DEATH & BREATH
THE 5 STEP GRIEF PROCESS

Are these questions familiar? Have you ever asked yourself such questions in times of sorrow, sadness or   personal tragedy and loss?

How do you handle the premature departure of a beloved, a friend, sister, brother, mother or father? How about a pet, a dog, cat or bird?

What feelings do you experience around a mass shooting, an accident, an earthquake or tsunami, or perhaps at the funeral of a young child taken away too early? What about visiting a memorial such as Hiroshima in Japan or the Killing Fields in Cambodia?

One could ask why is there so much pain, sorrow, and grief? Why so much suffering, so much injustice, so many tragedies?

Death has been a big part of my life since I was five years old when my cousin died from drowning on a school trip. My naive interpretation was that he was going to be a star or a guide and we would still be able to communicate with him - just differently. "He's not really gone, he has simply changed shape, and if we wanted to communicate with him, we can simply say a prayer, or talk and communicate with him in other ways."

I remember my mother, aunt and uncle looking at me as if I was an alien being when I shared my experience. I remember walking away, shaking my head, and wondering "why do they prefer to cry, moan and suffer from my cousin's transition?"

Fast forward to 2019, my first year back in Canada after over thirty years living in Japan, Singapore and Hong Kong. Within a short time, I was greeted with two aunties, my mother's bird and the family dog, all transitioning.

My curiosity with death, transitioning and passing over has been a fascinating exploration into culture, religion, and spirituality for over fifty years. I have studied, taught and interviewed mediums, psychics, and spiritual guides, and my beliefs have assisted me in dealing with grief and trauma, as well as introducing me to study trans-generational trauma, the Akashic records, neuroscience and the occult.

My experience with death was transformed when I was in Pune, the Osho Ashram, where we did an exercise in honoring the life and death of a single breath.

In this exercise, I invite you to find a quiet place away from any machine operated devices such as cars, trucks or planes. Allow yourself three to five minutes to explore your relationship with breath.

1. In a quiet environment, place your feet gently on the floor, or if you prefer you can lie down on your back in a comfortable resting position. Close your eyes and notice your breath.

2. With each breath, inhale and exhale, noticing the subtle movements in your body, Breathe in through your nose and exhale through your mouth or nose - it is your choice.

3. After 3-5 normal breaths, I invite you to breathe in deeply, filling your lungs to near capacity, and noticing the expansion of your chest, observing the sensations of your expanded chest, shoulders and lower back. As you exhale, exhale with heightened awareness to approximately 70 - 90% full exhalation, noticing your reactions and responses to a conscious exhalation.

4. Continue to breathe, noticing the fullness of your inhalation and fullness of your exhalation. At an apex of the inhalation, hold the breath for an additional 2-5 seconds and then slowly exhale. Notice your response, reaction and send an honoring message of 'thank you' or a specific sense of gratitude to the breath as it

oxygenates your blood, as it expands your breathing capacity, as it brings life force into your body and brings a new reference point to your amazing abilities to connect to the cosmos.

5. As you exhale slowly and fully, notice your chest contract, your shoulders shift, and the release of the breath. As you feel emptiness and lack of air, hold the sensation for an additional 2-5 seconds and notice no breath, as the breath dissolves into the ether. The state of no breath or no air is a feeling to explore, to observe and notice your reaction or response to this state of being.

6. What do you experience in the gap between a new breath and the full expulsion or death of the breath? Do you experience fear? Is it worry? Is it panic? Is it anxiety? Or is it calm? Is it peace? Is it tranquility?

7. Practice this exercise daily, weekly or monthly. Explore the changes in your relationship with your breath. It is your life force. It does regulate whether you live or die. Few people explore their relationship with their breath, and fewer people embrace the lessons that conscious breathing can deliver to enhance the ups and downs of life, the meanings that we give to life's experience and to the miracles that we can witness daily.

"Breath is your life, and breath is also the bridge between the conscious and the unconscious, between your body and soul. The bridge has to be used."

~ Vedas

21 ++ Ways to Experience Breathing

Breathe and notice calm

Breathe and feel connected

Breathe and sigh....'ahhhhh'

Breathe, smile, and say 'yes' softly

Breathe and release a sense of hurt

Breathe and pump your fist and say 'yes' loudly

Breathe, think funny thoughts and giggle

Breathe and send gratitude to your best friend

Breathe and express appreciation to someone who gifted you with a learning experience

Breathe and welcome new beginnings

Breathe an inner smile and say 'thank you' to a beloved who has passed on

Breathe and have a little kind chat with your maker

Breathe and extend your spine - imagine an imaginary string is extending the crown of your head to the ceiling

Breathe and let go of an old scar of regret

Breathe and surrender to your genius

Breathe and think of cute puppies or kittens and say 'ahhh'

Breathe and send energetic caring hugs to a former lover or friend.

Breathe and imagine peaceful spooning with your favorite friend

Breathe and say 'WOW' as you see an incredible sunrise

Breathe and step into your bravery

Breathe and feel an inside out hug as you witness a sunrise that inspires a deep sense of awesomeness

Breathe and feel ready to sleep

Breathe and be inspired to eat nutritiously

Breathe and do 50 squats

CASE STUDY - One Response To Death

GRIEF LETTER TO MY TRIBE

Dear Tribe,

Heartfelt condolences to the family, friends, classmates, teachers, and to everyone impacted by the earthquake that struck Malaysia's Mount Kinabalu this past Friday morning. I feel a deep sense of sadness for the families of the six Singapore primary school students and a teacher who were on an excursion to the peak and among those killed when the 6.0 magnitude quake struck Friday morning.

An eyewitness noted that "boulders 'the size of cars' rolled down the crowded slopes of Malaysia's Mount Kinabalu after the earthquake," as authorities on Sunday raised the death toll in the disaster to 16.

As I experience a sense of sadness, I am reminded of the disaster in Nepal (which killed over 8,800 people and injured 23,000 people), and my son's experiences with his school trips to Nepal and Malaysia over the past few years. This feeling brings to mind a very useful therapist tool that I have used over the years in my coaching and mentoring practice.

The Kübler-Ross Model can be used in a wide variety of situations of personal loss, such as the death of a loved one, the loss of a job or income, rejection, the end of a relationship or divorce, incarceration, and the onset of disease, infertility and even minor losses.

May this sharing assist the members of the TRIBE, and please do feel free to share with friends and family in times of need.

The stages are popularly known by the acronym DABDA

Stage 1 **DENIAL** — One of the first reactions is denial, wherein the survivor imagines a false, preferable reality.

Stage 2 **ANGER** - When an individual realizes that denial cannot continue, they become frustrated, especially at proximate individuals. Certain psychological responses of a person undergoing this phase would be: "Why me? It's not fair!"; "How can this happen to me?"; "'Who is to blame?"; "Why would God let this happen?"

Stage 3 **BARGAINING** - The third stage involves the hope that the individual can avoid a cause of grief. Usually, the negotiation for an extended life is made with a higher power in exchange for a reformed lifestyle. Other times, they will use anything valuable against another human agency to extend or prolong a life. People facing less serious trauma can bargain or seek compromise.

Stage 4 **DEPRESSION** - "I'm so sad, why bother with anything?"; "I'm going to die soon so what's the point?"; "I miss my loved one, so why go on?" During the fourth stage, the individual becomes saddened by the certainty of death. In this state, the individual may become silent, refuse visitors and spend much of the time mournful and sullen.

Stage 5 **ACCEPTANCE** - "It's going to be okay."; "I can't fight it, I may as well prepare for it." In this last stage, individuals embrace mortality or inevitable future, or that of a loved one, or other tragic events. People dying may precede the survivors in this state, which typically comes with a calm, retrospective view for the individual, and a stable condition of emotions.

MY EXPERIENCE - Soul Journey

For the past fifteen years, I have co-led Soul Journey sacred trips to amazing energetically charged places like Egypt, Peru & Bolivia, Mexico, South Africa, Japan-China-Korea, as well as Scotland, France, India, Scandinavia and Cambodia.

During these soul journeys, I have been blessed and honored to share personal coaching sessions relating to trauma, guilt and loss.

During the healing process, I invite the survivor of extreme experiences to explore their feelings, emotions and interpretations of their most emotionally charged experiences. I explain the Kübler-Ross Model to them, primarily so they can become familiar with a model that may assist them with their grieving process and thereby let go of some of the pain, explore alternative perspectives and alleviate blame, guilt or doubt from their current interpretations. A fresh perspective or alternative meaning may be the secret sauce to their highly personal healing or grieving process.

I assist them to explore their feelings and invite them to delve consciously into their emotional guidance system as well as invite them to discover or possibly find a GIFT, Sacred Message or Divine Lesson arising from the hurtful experience, the pain of an untimely death, or even a heinous crime, brutality or betrayal.

I call this process "TRAGIC INTO MAGIC" and it is a methodology where I respectfully invite the individual to delve deeply into their spirit, explore their ancestral memories and discover their belief constructs around religion, guides, gods, deities and even their divinity or higher purpose.

The timing of the shift from "tragic to magic " is personal and dependent upon the individual. While I have witnessed an immediate shift in some people, I am particularly respectful to the healing, the grieving process, and predominately the divine timing that is a hugely important element in honoring the personal journey for each person that I connect with.

When one takes action for others, one's own suffering is transformed into the energy that can keep one moving forward; a light of hope illuminating a new tomorrow for oneself and others is kindled.
~ Daisaku Ikedu

The wound is the place
where the light
enters you.
~ Rumi

How do you remain vibrant, refreshed and focussed?

LONELINESS, OVERWHELM AND CORPORATE PTSD
ARE THESE DIRTY WORDS IN YOUR CORPORATE CULTURE?

According to Harvard Business Review (HBR), half of all CEOs express feelings of loneliness, 61% of whom believe loneliness hinders their performance.

The office environment is intense enough, yet when you add in the impact of making extremely tough decisions under the magnifying glass of the media, stakeholders and technology, the phrase, "It's lonely at the top" has never been more relevant.

What is the approach to remain vibrant, refreshed and focussed on the tasks ahead?

In 2019, the basketball world witnessed the concept of Load Management, as Kawhi Leonard and the 2019 World Champion Toronto Raptors marched to dethroning the 5-time championship bound and two-time defending champions, The Golden State Warriors. By utilizing a long-practiced, yet seldom mastered approach, they focussed on managing the time, and physical and mental stress of their leading superstar and playoff Most Valuable Player (#MVP), Kawhi Leonard.

CEOs are now seen as public figures more so than ever before, yet unlike the public figures in the sports world, where is load management in the corporate world?

Does it exist? What about corporate stress disorder or Corporate PTSD? Is this indeed a reality in the corporate playing arena?

Can you imagine the mental, physical and social stress of a 24/7 position, 365 days of the year?

The HBR study revealed that 50% of chief executive officers (CEOs) have reported feeling a sense of loneliness. On top of that, 61% felt that it held them back from delivering their best at work. The problem is particularly acute in international postings due to the added complexities of varying work cultures, global time changes and head office-centric approaches to operating a global enterprise.

Global Shutdown and Managing Expectations

Looking inside-out for growth across the survey, there rang a general theme of hunkering down, as CEOs adapt to the strongly nationalist and populist sentiment sweeping the globe.

The threats they consider most pressing are less existential (e.g. terrorism, climate change), and more related to the ease of doing business in the markets where they operate. Overregulation, policy uncertainty, lack of availability of key skills, and trade conflicts are all having an impact. When asked to identify the most attractive foreign markets for investment, CEOs are narrowing their choices and expressing more uncertainty.

Uncertainty has been magnified in 2020 as the pandemic known as COVID-19 has forced every business leader to make hard decisions that will cast devastating financial impact throughout 2020, and into the foreseeable future.

According to World Economic Forum, the outbreak of COVID-19 highlights;

- Cracks in global trust, the pitfalls of global interdependency and the challenge for global governance.

- Epidemics are both a stand-alone business risk and an amplifier of existing trends and vulnerabilities.

- Businesses that invest in strategies for operational and financial resilience to emerging global risks, will be better positioned to respond and recover.

- Pandemics are now at the top of national risk-management frameworks in many countries.

Beyond standard concerns related to business operational continuity, employee protection and market preservation, businesses – and countries – must take a fresh look at their exposure to complex and evolving inter-dependencies. And it's CEOs, and those in high-ranking positions, who are called upon to carry the load of the compounding effects of pandemics and other crises.

In a recent podcast, I was asked for some insights or ways to engage and shine a light on Corporate PTSD. "Greg & Nate's World," is a podcast focusing on challenging conversations, heightening awareness in a wide range of mental health issues, including Corporate PTSD, as well as promoting and appreciating diversity and leadership.

The co-hosts, Greg, a mental health therapist, and Nate, a military veteran, who was diagnosed with PTSD as a result of his deployment in the Middle East, asked me to share some ways that may help overcome loneliness, develop self-leadership and discover some effective load management approaches for leaders.

> No man will make a great leader who
> wants to do it all himself.
> ~ Andrew Carnegie

Load Management Strategies

1. Remain Calm - Communicate Clearly

In the wake of crisis management, pandemic or natural disasters, the leader must remain calm, especially in public and communicate with accurate and up-to-date information.

In the background, the leader must find ways to alleviate the pressure and stresses of the position and set up a routine that lends support to both physical and mental expression. It's important to schedule vitality time, such as exercise and nutrition, as a top priority in your weekly plan. Invest time in your well-being and it will lead to increased resourcefulness in dealing with challenges that arise.

Explore ways to bring a dynamic balance to your daily or weekly regime

2. Be Realistic

Be aware and familiar with various options to take action around risk parameters, as well as being open to worst-case scenario planning. Managing expectations by clearly articulating worst-case scenarios, followed by best-case scenarios, will add credibility and confidence.

Deriving practical and productive plans to move forward, will determine what steps can be undertaken and executed to deliver what is promised.

3. Be Authentic.

Being sincere and authentic encourages honest conversation, fosters discussion and invites adaptability, flexibility, and collaboration in dealing with crisis management. A balanced scorecard in authentic leadership measures self-awareness, genuineness, fair-mindedness and doing the right thing.

4. Nurture Your Team

Be the example of self-care first and invite associates to know that it is ok to seek assistance and help. Develop approaches and tools to help people to stay flexible, out of danger, and encourage a sense of teamwork and collaboration, even if quarantined or working remotely for a prolonged period. Stack activities that can bring learning, nurturing and connecting. Develop new approaches to existing activities that present playful, light, and innovative approaches to your existing situations or rituals.

Explore ways and strategies to assist with your practice of being present in the moment. From deep mindful breathing to yoga and meditation, to more physically intensive activities such as swimming, running, or biking, tackle activities that allow you to get away from the office and release endorphins that will re-set the mind, body and spirit.

If it ain't broke, don't fix it might not be the optimal approach. We might invite the question, *"What could we do better to make this experience even better?"* This may be a question for incremental or monumental improvements.

Letting your team know you're open to discussing important issues will make them feel more comfortable coming to you. Explore how you are feeling and expressing yourself in the boardroom, and the household.

Allow and invite others to cultivate trust, respect, and pathways to overcome loneliness and isolation. If you are confiding in others and let them truly see you, you are breaking the barriers of isolation and encouraging the conversations that come with the corporate battlefield.

Leaders must evolve and implement approaches that integrate key learnings, infuse creativity and foster collaborative change into their personal and professional life.

INTO THE DISCOURSE

As the global pandemic virus known today as Covid-19 surges around the globe, it is an increasingly complex world of uncertainty wherein self-isolation, physical distancing, and our professional and personal lives are being disrupted.

Perhaps, by adapting best practices from professional sports such as load management, we may find new approaches or possibilities for life and discover that it doesn't always have to be lonely at the top.

Compassion, curiosity and connection could be part of the great global re-set as a pathway to bring the champion approach to building world-class enterprises.

Perhaps, authentic conversation, nurturing support groups, and taking time to reconnect with nature or oneself will be a reset from Covid-19.

Let's explore the possibilities.

What will you do to overcome the loneliness of forced self-isolation?

What can we do to engage Corporate PTSD with compassion?

What are the top three areas for your personal and professional mental wellness positivity plan for the next year?

What is a passion project you can start this month?

As I left the podcast environment in St. Thomas, Ontario, I was reminded of Nate's comment of him noticing hundreds of Canadians driving their vehicles for sixty to ninety minutes per day, in a half-zombie, half-comatose state, hating and despising their life.

The innovation and invitation here is to identify one idea, one thought, or one new approach and apply it. Take a step to do something new, embrace a new word, a new thought or a new action. Infuse this approach into your daily regime and notice the shift in your energy, your resilience and your positivity. I welcome your insights and feedback and invite you to explore, experiment and express.

EXPLORE THE WELLNESS WAY
- An Ode To Loneliness, Overwhelm and Corporate PTSD In A Disruptive World

Age 27 in Tokyo, my life was go go go
I was an ex-pat banker with all the trimmings to show

On the outside all looked great
Yet stress, insomnia and self-doubt my heart, it ate

My colleague cracked up and dissolved in front of me
He lost over 30 kg in his tenure, for all to see

Stress, panic attacks and Corporate PTSD is real, you know
Self-esteem and confidence shrinks, self-doubt starts to grow

Worry, fear and doubt, insomnia peaks
Cold sweats, nightmares, sleep apnea leaks

Two out of three will be hit with mental illness and disease
For me It was terrible, horrible, it beat me to my knees

Suicide was calling, imagined falling 13 floors
Paranoia, alcohol, medication, addiction, there were no doors

Screaming for help, I did get
An experience, I will never forget

Altered states, fogginess and roads I did steer
My steps while uncertain, they unfolded so clear

First change the input, eat greens, fruits and daily I walked
Cut alcohol, soda pop and sugars, I so, self-talked

Start learning and researching and finding a way
Changing words, focus and start to play

Talked to my boss on ways to heal
To our leaders, we must make a strong and bold appeal

My life was saved, it was by the grace of God
Shifting my life, delivered me from the firing squad

Stress, Panic Attacks and Corporate PTSD is real, you see
Look up, look down, look around, it is not only me

One, two, three or seven steps may work for you
No need to pay thousands, feel alone or sit in a queue

Step 1) Eat green, eat fresh nourishing food for your health
Step 2) Walk, stretch and movement is true wealth
Step 3) Sunlight, Vitamin D and nature fuels the soul
Step 4) Positive attitude, prayer meditation,
            perhaps a singing bowl
Step 5) Self-study, be curious and discover the plan for you
Step 6) Sharing, caring and service for others may provide
            THE clue
Step 7) Last and not least might be write write write
            A diary or journal may help you see what the light

Healing, caring, kind words for you and me
Be present, be pure, be progress for all to see

Start today with a thought or caring verse
To plant a seed, nurture love, let's rehearse

Awareness, compassion and caring ways to bring order to this
mess
Healthy word medicine, curiosity and self-discovery for
corporate PTSD and stress

Corporate PTSD thank you for this day
Fuel the healthy mind, nurture a healing heart and explore
The Wellness Way

Are you feeling lost? Confused?
Lethargic or Low energy?

DISCOVER YOUR
TRUE NORTH

Before jumping into a barrage of medical tests and embarking on a pharmaceutical pathway, let's explore a five-step process to discover and calibrate your daily, weekly and monthly activities utilizing your true north.

What does True North mean?

The term True North is used in sailing to know where you are and where you want to go.

It is a star-centric navigational approach that sailors have used for millennia and removes considerable stress, pressure and uncertainly in life.

Wouldn't it be empowering to feel guided, connected and directed with certainty, confidence and flexibility? To explore your life journey with a personal calibration system that keeps you on track, yet also enables you to explore, deviate and innovate without feeling regret, waste, or worse, feeling stupid, lost or alone.

True North is as easy as looking up into the sky at night, calibrating with the stars, and connecting with your present point, noticing the brightest stars and then triangulating with a third point, to give you a directional focus or bearing, that allows you to confidently step forward with 2020 vision, curiosity and confidence.

Embrace your personal True North, as it is yours, and yours alone. It is not your mom's, your dad's, your aunt's or your uncle's, or your best friend's.   And guess what?

True North can change as you change,
it can evolve as you evolve and
it adjusts as you adjust

True North is not about being right or wrong. It is about 2020 vision and embracing the idea that your next step is right or left, not right or wrong. True North isn't about a step forward or a step backward, it is about stepping into life, growing or moving like a traveler, an explorer, or a life-long learner.

Do you like to travel?

Ever wonder why you like to travel?

If you answered 'yes', write down ten reasons you like to travel?

_____

_____

_____

Perhaps you wrote answers like:

I like to travel because ....
I like to explore
I like to experiment with food
I like to study different cultures
I like to meet new people
I feel free
I don't have to work
I get to learn

If your answers are similar, terrific, if not, let's continue and explore what else we can discover with our True North experiment.

I would like to propose another rationale behind your joy of traveling. Perhaps you like traveling because you like who you *are* as a traveler.

Yes!
You like you as a traveler
You like that you are outgoing
You like you as a curious seeker
You like you as a friendly, kind, and humble adventurer

You like your willingness to ask questions, to be flexible and adapt to changing environments.

Ultimately you really like who you are as a traveler

So let's gather these qualities and infuse them into our daily lives and let's live life consistently with these inspiring qualities.

Knowing your True North gives you a navigation system that supports you 24/7, 365 days a year and provides you with 2020 vision to live your life with certainty, confidence and with enough curiosity and adventure to keep your life fresh, fun and fantabulous.

Let's get started on your True North
calibration system

STEP 1

Nurture a healthy, abundant attitude around gratitude. Write a list of ten, twenty or fifty things in your life that you are grateful for?

If this is an easy exercise for you, congratulations, and continue to nurture a healthy attitude of gratitude.

If this was a difficult challenge, let's look at some different ways to be grateful.

Can you be grateful for your wellness?
For your Country?
For your family?
For your mind?
For your ingenuity?
For your friends?
For your ability to communicate?
For being able to read?
For being able to write?
For your teachers?
For the obstacles that developed your resilience?

The attitude of gratitude is about being present. It is about noticing what you can influence right now and it is about honoring the current situation.

Exploring your True North from a point of gratitude, yields incredible benefits of being resourceful, being innovative and tapping into your higher powers of intuition, connectedness and positivity.

2020 Vision is realized when you develop the habit, muscle memory, and the personalized calibration system that starts with getting yourself into a state of gratitude.

Having the questions, the perspective and the process to get yourself into a state of gratitude will be a game-changer in your life.

To support your effectiveness of being able to move from any state into a state of gratitude, the visual below can be used daily to deal with the ups and downs of everyday living. This model is called Above The Line / Below The Line.

OAR

BED

Living above the line is as if you have an OAR that will assist you to navigate life's obstacles, challenges and opportunities.

The R stands for Responsibility and to play life above the line, you must learn to take personal Responsibility for any situation, as well as have the ability to Respond to the situation with resourcefulness, confidence and a willingness to do your best.

The A in OAR stands for Accountability, and playing life above the line is about having a self-respect, self-awareness and Accountability to self and to others. Top performers have a high sense of accountability and are willing to dig deep to deliver stellar results.

The O stands for Ownership and top performers take ownership of their situation, their life and their emotional state. To live above the line, you must Own your emotions and be able to make changes to steer your ship in the direction that will yield the optimal result. Asking quality questions, focussing on the solution, and being present to the situation are all ways to take ownership, be resourceful and be a victor in life.

Living life below the line is a metaphor that can be easily identified, consumes huge quantities of energy and creates a heavy, helpless, victim mindset.

The acronym is BED, and I suggest staying in, rather than getting out of bed if your inner voice is sounding like any of the key characters who reside below the line.

The D stands for doubt. The voice you hear from the doubter is a whiny, mocking and pitiful voice that doubts that you can do it, make it, or complete it. It reminds you of being in your most un-resourceful state. When doubt takes over the conversation in your head, you can counteract with, "But what if you could?" I like to remember a quote from my dear friend and tour guide, Mr. V from Cambodia, who says "never try, never know." Or you can invite gratitude into your self-talk conversations and ask, "What could I be grateful for from this situation?" By shifting the dialogue away from the 'doubter' you reclaim your power and move from below the line to above the line, tapping into your personal responsibility.

The E stands for Excuses, or as I refer to it, the number one illness of the spirit of possibilities. What excuses do you use to clog your opportunities, possibilities, or living above the line? Is your inner voice stuck with excuses? 'I'm too old.' 'I'm too young.' 'I'm not smart enough, tall enough, good enough.' What are the excuses you tell yourself? Are you willing to stop playing small and be willing to tap into your greatness? Can you explore your potential and step above the line by being grateful for the opportunity to embrace new perspectives?

Finally, the B in BED stands for Blame and it is probably the number one reason people choose to live life below the line. Blame your parents, your teachers, your ethnicity, your age, your weight, your color, your education. What do you blame and what self-talk is keeping you and your life small?

By using this process, you can shift your self-talk, embrace the attitude of gratitude and start living above the line, immediately.

One of my mentors and coaches, Tony Robbins, suggests, "Change your questions, change your perspective, change your information, and you will change your destiny."

By transforming your self-talk, with this process of embracing the attitude of gratitude, and by living above the line, rather than below it, will be a brilliant starting point to live with 2020 Vision and opens up the amazing forces, possibilities and opportunities coming together for you in your life, starting NOW!

OWNERSHIP
ACCOUNTABILITY
RESPONSIBILITY

BLAME
EXCUSES
DOUBT

This invites the metaphor of living above the line or below the line and by establishing **gratitude** as a solid foundation of your life journey. It also provides a wonderful metaphor to notice when you are stuck in an un-resourceful cycle or living below the line.

By nurturing a strong sense of gratitude, it provides you with a powerful foundation of resilience and adaptability to deal with life's challenges.

An attitude of gratitude accelerates the ability to adapt, shift or pivot in times of challenge and infuses the "CAN DO" attitude in ways to solve problems, and explore opportunities and possibilities.

If your true north global positioning system starts with Gratitude, it provides you with a perspective from inner strength, power and flexibility.

STEP 2
Tapping into your TRUE NORTH explores your life purpose and passions.

If you were to answer the question, what is your purpose?
My purpose is …..

_____

And what are you passionate about?
I am passionate about….

_____

When faced with these questions, I have noticed that more than 70% of people struggle with one or both of these questions. If you have your answers, I congratulate you as your True North will enable you to infuse your purpose and passion in a regular, consistent and nurturing manner.

For those of you who might find these questions difficult to answer, the following exercise is designed to assist you to lighten up, loosen up and let go with some curiosity, exploration and practice.

In designing a practical method for finding your True North, I ask you to explore the following questions.

For purpose, the questions are:

What do you like?

What would you like to study or learn?

What hobbies do you enjoy?

Start doing what you like in a methodical and practical manner *immediately*.

Do things you like to do. Stop delaying or postponing things that you want to study or would like to learn about.

A big component of following your True North is getting into the mindset of learning, and by being in a learning space, we shift into an arena of vulnerability, curiosity and personal and professional growth.

This growth component is essential in finding and following your True North.

For passion, let's answer the questions:

What do you love to do?

What do you really enjoy doing, or used to enjoy, that was stopped when you were young?

What would you love to do, besides traveling, if you had ten million dollars in the bank?

Perhaps a parent or teacher told you to stop doing something because you 'could not make a living' playing piano, painting or dancing?

By exploring our 'loves' or passions, and by starting to rekindle a sense of active joy, passion or delight, we energize our spirit to shine bright and can activate the four major chemicals in our brain that influence our happiness. A DOSE of amazement can deliver a healthier, happier, and more inspired you for the world to experience.

Ever wondered why young people are enamored by gaming and interactive online activities? Would it surprise you that the brain is stimulated by a combination of chemicals, and in particular, the way that DOSE is stimulated?

D is for Dopamine, and is what we normally think of as the 'happiness' drug. However, this is a big misconception. Dopamine is actually involved more with the anticipation than the actual 'happiness' feeling. Dopamine is often described as a striving emotion.

Oxytocin is the O in DOSE and is the neurochemical that has allowed us to become social creatures. It makes us feel empathy, which helps us feel close and bonded to others. When released, Oxytocin is a mingling of trust and physical touch, as well as love-making.

Serotonin is the S in DOSE and if you're in a good mood, you've got Serotonin to thank. And if you're in a bad mood, you've got Serotonin to blame. It's a regulator of our happiness and approximately 80% of Serotonin exists in the gut, and is governed by our state of 'hunger.' We can stimulate Serotonin with sunlight, eating and physical movement.

The E in DOSE is for Endorphins, which are responsible for masking pain or discomfort. This explains their association with the 'fight or flight' response. When it comes to designing happiness, endorphins help you power through and can be triggered by vigorous exercise, laughter and physical movement.

In the gaming experience, game makers and online community leaders are setting up a time frame to bring learning, exploring and playing with your DOSE.

In the GPS Calibration System, we are inviting you to design your next 6-18 months with activities that give you frequent constructive feedback. Explore ways to give yourself more 'likes' and 'loves' and ways to stimulate you and your daily DOSE.

By practicing, remembering and exploring our purpose and passion, we can start to embrace the mindset of possibilities.

And by being willing to activate our mantra of living with purpose and passion, we can start exploring with consciousness and curiosity, that which allows us to live with purpose and passion on a daily basis, rather than walking around saying things such as;

" I don't know my purpose"
"I don't know what I am passionate about"
" I am so lost"

True North is enabled when we bring together the consciousness of words, the practical experiments of conscious living, and the intersection of infusing daily activities towards growth, learning and practicing wellness and mindfulness.

STEP 3

Let's triangulate **Gratitude** and **Purpose & Passion** with the third component, **Service**. The questions to explore are:

Who would you enjoy serving, helping and guiding?

With ten million in the bank, what group, or interest groups, would you like to make a difference for?

It could be living green, living healthier or serving seniors, newborns, differently-abled or anyone and anything in between.

Service is the component of our True North where we can wait until we retire. Or we could start today with a small donation, some volunteering or with some projects that infuse service and contribution into our TRUE NORTH journey.

We invite you to find ways to be of service today, yet the milestone maybe something to set as a goal with a three-year time horizon. By having time to plan and discuss, the doing can have incredible results that can unfold just by getting started.

CASE STUDY - Power of Small

In 2007, a group of small business owners had an idea. We asked, "What would happen if we all gave back just by doing the things we do every day?" It was a question that deeply inspired us. Three years and a great undertaking later, a smaller group of inspired social entrepreneurs led by Masami Sato and her team, were able to design the systems and processes necessary to make it work, and the dream is now a reality.

The initiative was originally called 'BUY 1 GIVE 1,' backed by the idea that companies would make a giving impact with each designated business transaction. Today, the B1G1 initiative has more than 2,600 businesses from around the world, each making significant impacts every day.

B1G1 is a social enterprise and non-profit organization with a mission to create a world full of giving. The giving can be services, products and contributions. Unlike conventional giving models, B1G1 helps small and medium-sized businesses to achieve more social impact by embedding giving activities into everyday business operations and creating unique giving stories. Every business transaction (and as a result, the businesses' everyday activity) can impact lives for as little as just one cent.

Masami Sato is the epitome of what we refer to as the Power of Small - she may not be tall but she found a GPS calibration system that exemplifies gratitude, aligned with inspiring purpose and passion, sprinkled with daily service and contribution.

Masami is the guiding light behind almost every project at B1G1, from IT design, to project management, to guiding culture. Masami is one of the most humble, engaging, and inspiring people you'll ever meet.

She has traveled around the globe to more than 30 countries, across 5 continents, and her experiences have given her a unique perspective on life and giving. Masami has an uncanny ability to help others see things from a different perspective - a wonderful, inspiring perspective.

To learn more about how B1G1 may assist you, or your business to start serving or contributing today as part of your personalized calibration system, kindly check out;

www.B1G1.com

SMALL BUSINESSES CAN CHANGE THE WORLD IN A BIG WAY

SIMPLE AS; 1 - 2 - 3 OR G - P - S

1. Start with being grateful, right now, in this moment.
2. Be aware of learning, enjoying and acting from gratitude, knowing that it is applying your likes and loves to your purpose and passion.
3. Know that you are in service to humanity, to our planet, to our cosmos. Know that you are making a difference and operate from this collective TRUE NORTH triangulated perspective.

Like the navigator on the sea, you can use the GPS Global Positioning System to become your personal True North guidance system.

By being present with gratitude, by stepping forward daily, purposefully and passionately, and with a knowingness that you are serving, encouraging or nurturing others, your first steps forward will be coming from the 2020 vision perspective.

2020 Vision is about taking the first step forward and then enjoying the momentum that results when one is aligned and energized, with a personal GPS calibration system.

2020 Vision is not about knowing what will happen weeks, months, years and decades in the future. It is about bringing the clear, confident and joyful you to the world.

Does this sound simple?
Fun?
Exciting?

INVITATION

Hopefully the old or existing mental framework is ready to be set aside, shelved or consciously placed on a permanent leave of absence, and we can choose to reformat, redesign and reboot with a new level of awareness, articulation and experience.

Are you ready to update habits, beliefs and disempowering words with innovation, inspiration and insightful initiatives?

If so, it is time, a divine time to embrace the 2020 Vision and utilize the Gratitude, Purpose & Passion, and Service Calibration System to step forward into a new reality.

A reality that you connect to your higher self, you step forward collaborating, embracing and exploring your Passion and Purpose and you co-create a Brave New World in service and commitment to your 2020 Vision today and each day forward.

I invite you to become
not just a coach,
but an
Awesome Impact Coach

HOW TO USE THIS BOOK

In 2020, consultants and professional trainers know that traditional methods, including devising a solution and telling people what to do, just doesn't work very well.

However, facilitating change, asking questions, engaging people, obtaining a buy-in and commitment, now that delivers results. That is what coaching is all about, proactively helping people and companies to move from their current state of being to their desired state.

During a typical coaching workshop, I ask participants to smile, exchange a high five with the person next to them and then say "You are AWESOME!" Ok, this might sound a bit weird or touchy-feely. You might even say "That's so American!" (Reminder: I'm from the country with the maple leaf on its flag, not the stars and stripes). But the energy in the room is instantly transformed. The participants start to relax, laugh and giggle and become more receptive to learning something new.

Try it. Say "Awesome." Say it right now. "AWESOME!" Your mouth actually needs to contort and shift to say the word. With just a little added energy and enthusiasm, this contortion can shift your state of being and empower your entire physiology. Words have power. See what happens today, if you decide to answer the question "How are you?" with "AWESOME" instead of your normal response.

One of my students tried this for a week. Not only did she feel better inside, but her colleagues started calling her "that awesome lady."

This book is also about

IMPACT

Everything that happens in the world around us leaves an impression. Whether this impact is positive or negative depends on our mastery of emotions.

Impacts move us, sometimes physically, and sometimes mentally, from one state to another. A coach needs to make an impact in order to be a catalyst for transformation.

Whether you read "Awesome Impact Coach" in a single sitting or a chapter at a time, it's also important to be ACTIVE.

Don't just watch from the stands. Do the exercises at the end of each chapter. Participate. Coaching is a practical application. You need to apply what you read.

Start a journal of your coaching process. In fact, go grab a notebook right now. Write down the date and time. Begin to record the highlights of each session and ideas that have made an impression on you and the steps required to follow up.

Keeping a journal will not only track your progress, but will also accelerate your learning.

The best venue to bring these lessons into the workplace is at a weekly staff or project meeting.

Choose one chapter each week and allocate 15 minutes to discuss it. Let your team decide if an idea resonates with them.

Not every strategy works for everyone

The tools that impact your associates may differ from the ones that work best for you. However, if your team can embrace a lesson from **just one chapter**, your sales will go up.

Bold statement I know, but implement and embrace some of the strategies in this book and you will see a difference! Office morale will rise and you'll notice that the people around you are energized, enthusiastic and more willing to take on challenges personally designed for them.

You'll have succeeded in bringing Awesome Impact Coaching, a process of continuous change and growth, into your workplace.

Have fun and enjoy the coaching process

The key to the development of
your coaching competence...

... is to start

Power is in your words.
Use the word AWESOME
and it will BE part of your being!

YOU ARE AN AWESOME IMPACT COACH!

How do you become an awesome impact coach?

Here are the initial steps:

First, while reading this book, practice the exercises and action steps suggested in each of the sections. Coaching is practical; you can only get better by applying what you read. Upon completion of this book and its action steps, you will have mastered many of the skills used by an awesome impact coach.

Second, begin to write a journal or a logbook to record highlights of your coaching sessions. Record the date, the results achieved, what you have learned, and the required follow up actions. The discipline involved in keeping a journal will accelerate your learning by effectively tracking your progress.

Third, **enjoy the coaching process**, the learning, the insights, and the ability to improve communication in the workplace.

In the beginning, it may appear that you spend considerable time preparing for the coaching sessions. However, as your abilities are elevated, your preparation time will decrease, and your efforts will contribute to empowering the coaching environment in the workplace.

An environment, which supports coaching, will permeate each and every associate. As you develop your coaching toolkit, you will notice that people around you are energized, enthusiastic, and more willing to take up challenges personally designed for them.

Quality Questions - Awesome Impact Coach

What qualities does an awesome impact coach have?

_____

_____

_____

Rate yourself as an awesome impact coach, 0 is horrible or terrible, 10 is outstanding?

Rating _____

What three specific steps can you take to move towards "being" an awesome impact coach in the next twenty-one days?

1) _____

2) _____

3) _____

A willingness and openness to learn
encourages creative input and
the sharing of new ideas

WILLINGNESS TO LEARN & LEAD

You have just taken a new position and everyone in the office expects you to have all the "right answers." The previous boss was autocratic; he told everyone what to do and made all the decisions.

Your approach is different.
You are an awesome impact coach

The behavior of an awesome impact coach may take people by surprise. The boss told everyone what to do, the coach asks many questions. The boss made all the decisions, the coach builds consensus. The boss fixed all the problems, the coach keeps problems from occurring. The boss blamed, the coach takes responsibility.

The awesome impact coach shares with the staff, their willingness to learn. This doesn't mean that a coach must be a buddy to all of the associates in the office, on the contrary, the coach is often ultimately responsible for ensuring the team's success. By accepting this responsibility, the coach shows they are willing to stretch, grow, and act as a role model for all associates.

To lead a team, firstly, the coach must find a careful balance between serving the needs of contributors and associates, while successfully ensuring they accomplish the goals or objectives within their roles.

Secondly, the coach must meet each of the team members individually for their first coaching session. Use this session to get to know your team by clarifying four areas:

- Current situation
- Current duties
- Who they work with
- What they would like their job to encompass in the future.

The answers to these questions will give you an insight into how you can work with your team to contribute to their overall learning.

Your new leadership style will encourage your team to adopt an energetic learning attitude

Their efficiency and productivity will increase and they will be open to learning new skills.

Here are useful suggestions to encourage a willingness to learn:

Be responsible. Take responsibility for your own learning and share information with others. Discuss courses or seminars you have attended, share books you have read, and suggest fun ways to enhance happiness, health and wellness in the workplace.

Be curious. Encourage curiosity in the workplace. Implement brainstorming or creativity sessions for the group to share their opinions or thoughts on improving productivity and efficiency.

Take the initiative. Don't wait for someone else to step up and take action. Join or start a speakers' club such as Toastmasters, invite a speaker to your office, take a course, explore new hobbies – be an active learner and share your learning with others in the office!

Quality Questions - Willingness to Learn

Rate yourself for learning and sharing in the workplace, 0 is horrible, 10 is outstanding

Rating _____

What three things can you do "even better" to nurture your learning and sharing in the workplace?

1) _____

2) _____

3) _____

If you take these actions in the next ten days, what would your rating be?

Rating _____

If your rating has increased, terrific, or; if not, what additional action can you take to improve your learning and sharing in the workplace?

_____

_____

_____

Asking for input creates an empowered environment based on respect and learning, and in turn generates great new possibilities

EMPOWERING ENVIRONMENT

How do you create an empowering environment in the workplace?

Many employed people will spend up to twelve hours of their day at work. A working environment often assumes the characteristics and qualities of the office leader or boss. Actions such as barking orders at subordinates, criticizing without reason, or tearing into fits of anger or rage, will contribute to creating an environment that is fueled by fear, doubt, and anxiety.

While these behaviors surely keep everyone on their toes, they likely have side effects such as high staff turnover, minimal creativity, high absenteeism and low work morale.

To create an empowering environment in the workplace, industry leaders must remove the old 'rule by fear' methods of the past, and replace them with the tools and principles of impact and empowering coaching.

Asking for input creates an empowered environment based on respect and learning, and in turn generates great new possibilities.

The new leaders are coaches and mentors who are committed to getting the very best out of themselves and their team. With an open mindset and a willingness to nurture an empowering environment, the coach shares challenges and opportunities with associates. They often ask for opinions on important, relevant and pertinent issues.

What does being a coach mean to you?

You may think of words such as caring, open, able, competent and helpful.

What other C O A C H words come to mind when you think of being an awesome impact coach?

When you ask for input, three great things happen even before you get the information.

- You show respect for your associates
- You don't assume you have all the answers
- You open up yourself and the office to new information and new possibilities

Ask empowering questions when you want to achieve open communication, increased information flow, and higher productivity.

How do you think we should handle it?
What do you think we should do?
What course of action do you believe would be best?

Here are my three tips to create an empowering environment in the workplace.

1. Create open communication by asking questions and listening to the associate's answers. This method takes a little bit longer than making all the decisions yourself, but it will create a climate where associates feel free to express themselves and suggest improvements.

2. Acknowledge other opinions and respect them. Make an effort to see things from the perspective of your associates because this will open your mind even more. You may not agree with all opinions, but you will learn more about your associates.

3. Consistency and persistence are essentials tools for nurturing an empowering coaching environment. Encourage everyone to coach and be coached on a regular basis. With heightened awareness and new skills, both individuals and the organization will be rewarded with increased productivity, efficiency and wellness in the office.

Quality Questions - Empowering Environment

On a scale of 0 to 10, 0 being terrible and 10 being outstanding, how do you rate yourself for contributing to an empowering environment at work?

Rating _____

What three actions could you take in the next week to make a positive difference in the workplace?

1) _____

2) _____

3) _____

If you take these actions in the next ten days, what would your rating be?

Rating _____

If your rating has increased, terrific, or; if not, what additional action can you take to improve your empowering environment?

_____

_____

_____

Don't make things complicated,
it's the simple ideas that are often
the most effective.
Keep It Simple and Smile– the KISS approach

SIMPLE APPROACH

Be simple!

In the simple approach to coaching, we look at the principle that "people like people like themselves." Because people tend to like people like themselves, the first step of the Simple approach to coaching is to identify some areas of similarity. Similarities include common language, common interests, and common company.

After establishing a common foundation, we can use the Simple approach to seek and gain permission to coach, facilitate and shift mindsets. Develop an approach to assist all and serve in the most direct manner.

The strength of the Simple approach lies in its ability to remove complexity and communicative obstacles. When we know where we are and where we want to go, we can develop the action steps needed to achieve the desired results. The Simple approach will facilitate smoother communication, more effective goal setting, and a higher probability of success.

Don't make things complicated.
It's the simple ideas that are often the most effective

The Simple approach to coaching depends on the ability of the coach to:

1. Identify the approach to which the associates will best respond.

2. Solicit the action plan from the associates.

3. Establish a high level of confidence or certainty that the actions will be completed.

4. Set up a reward and penalty system for completing an action, and for inaction.

5. Follow up using these simple attitudes: sincerity, interest, maturity, passion, love and empathy.

Throughout this book, we will continue to explore the components of the Simple approach to coaching. Simple does not necessarily mean easy. It takes great effort to master the concepts of simplicity, to express oneself in a simple yet elegant manner. Simplifying may require painstaking effort to express, describe and articulate meaning through words, voice quality and physiology.

Do this little exercise in "simplicity"

Can you tie your shoelaces? Of course! It is a simple process. But now describe how to tie the shoelaces and write it down in ten simple steps. Then, give it to someone and see if they can understand it!

Most people can tie their shoelaces but few people can describe the process with precision. Here are three great methods to achieve simplicity:

1. See things with new eyes, with young eyes and take a fresh approach to the task. Avoid stereotypes and complacency. Work with people in a simple, respectful manner.

2. Develop a habit of looking for easier ways to do things. Simplicity is a billion-dollar industry laced with structural engineers, logistic experts and management consultants all looking for ways to make things simpler.

3. Take responsibility for your "simple" message. If your message is not getting through, adapt your approach with other simple strategies, such as a diagram, a flow chart, a few words, or an analogy of how other persons describe their experiences to you. Ask yourself, how can we make this simpler?

Quality Questions - Simple Approach

Rate your ability to communicate simply and clearly in the workplace, 0 is not effective or horrible, while 10 is outstanding.

Rating _____

What three steps can you take to simplify your communication approach in the next thirty days?

1) _____

2) _____

3) _____

If these steps are implemented in the next thirty days, what would your rating be for simple and clear communication out of 10?

Rating _____

On a scale of 0 to 10, 0 not very committed and 10 absolutely committed, how committed are you to make it happen?

Rating _____

What would have to happen to make it an absolute must, a 10?

_____

_____

*Open your heart and allow yourself
to be vulnerable.
You will be amazed at the positive
results you will achieve.*

OPEN COMMUNICATION

During a recent workshop held in Singapore, one of the participants, a forty-something Chinese man, shared his experiences of raising his children. He rose, smiled, and in a barely audible voice told the audience that he was working so much that he scarcely knew his kids anymore.

Both he and his wife worked and their Indonesian domestic helper raised his two children aged five and seven. He found himself drifting away from his wife and his children. Time appeared so scarce to him, he felt he did not have time for himself, his wife, or his kids.

Most of the audience was nodding in agreement as if they knew exactly how this man was feeling.

As he continued to speak, he began to reflect on what and how he was communicating. All of a sudden he started to tear. He tried to stop himself, then suddenly became very apologetic and embarrassed by his display of emotion, and abruptly stopped talking.

I looked around the room and noticed quite a few wet eyes in the audience. I asked the man if he thought he was a good communicator. He shook his head, shrugged his shoulders and said, "No lah, I am Chinese educated, English not so good."

I asked him again, "Are you a good communicator?" He looked at me again and shook his head.

"No, lah, never speak in public before." I gently held up my hand and asked the class to raise their hands if they felt that the man was a good communicator. Everyone in the class raised their hands. We gave him a round of applause for his open sharing and impact communication.

Everyone in the room understood the man's message because he spoke from the heart. Opening your heart and sharing your message will often result in open communication.

An awesome impact coach practices open communication with discernment. This requires that you know your audience, sense your audience, and feel when it is appropriate to connect with your audience, at levels that may go deeper than day-to-day conversation. The awesome impact coach can use open communication while being alert to judge when the time and place are right for heart-felt communication.

Here are three ways to nurture open communication with discernment, in the workplace:

1.   Admit mistakes and offer a sincere, heartfelt apology to those who may be affected by your mistake. By admitting your mistakes, you can step up and accept responsibility for your actions and thereby keep open possibilities for deeper level communication.

2.   Keep your physiology open. Move your shoulders back, stretch your arms, look up into the sky and breathe. Positive physiology is contagious and contributes to greater health and wellness. It allows you to be more aware of your environment and to make wise choices about when to engage fellow workers in conversations that require deeper level open communication.

3.   Avoid absolute statements such as "everyone" or "nobody" or "all" - as in "everybody is against me", "nobody likes me" and "all guys are ruthless." These words are used often to exaggerate in a negative, weak and insincere manner.

When you communicate with people, it is not the length of the words you use that will achieve the desired results. It is the feeling, compassion or passion behind the words.

Quality Questions - Open Communication

Rate your ability to communicate with sincerity in the workplace? 0 is horrible, while 10 is outstanding?

Rating _____

In the next thirty days, what three steps can you take to communicate with sincerity "even better" in the workplace?

1) _____

2) _____

3) _____

If these steps are implemented in the next thirty days, what would your rating be for open and sincere communication out of 10?

Rating _____

The SMART Template is the ultimate
'CHANGE TOOL.'
Make sure your goals and strategies
are specific, measurable, achievable, relevant,
and have a time frame.

MEASURING WITH SMART

One of the most useful tools for an awesome impact coach is the template called the SMART system. Encourage and track results by introducing the SMART system into your coaching enterprise.

S stands for Specific.

Be specific in setting up your goal, objective or desired outcome. The more specific, clear and precise you are, the easier it is to elicit the support and power of the subconscious mind to develop a clear and effective strategy.

Clarity is power, so be specific with your goals

M is for Measurable.

Establish measurable parameters that can be easily gaged, tracked and compared against the desired outcomes. For example, a general goal would be to increase sales. A specific and measurable goal would be to increase sales by 15% in quarter four by contacting six new clients, following up on fifty existing clients and exploring at least three new business opportunities.

A is for Achievable.

Set achievable goals that will stretch you and enable you to grow. An awesome impact coach uses this component to assess the participant's confidence or level of certainty in achieving the desired outcomes.

The objective of the coach is to find out limiting beliefs or blockages that may be affecting confidence levels and holding the participants back from reaching their desired outcomes. The coach identifies various positive resources that the participants can access to increase their certainty of success.

These resources include using past experiences or successes to get the participant to visualize, feel, smell and taste the experience of being successful. With increased confidence the probability of taking the first step soars, momentum is created, and you start to develop a positive feedback loop.

R is for Relevance.

Are the goals relevant to the participant? In a workplace, aligning the goals so that both the organization and the associate both win, is essential to developing an effective coaching environment. Goals must be relevant to the associate or they will not work towards them. Creating an emotional attachment to goals is a way of making them relevant and desirable and is an effective method of achieving results.

Emotional attachment to goals can be created by accessing the emotional triggers of pain and pleasure to intensify the relevance of the goals being set. An awesome impact coach helps employ pleasure or works towards values, to establish a reward system for success.

The coach can also establish certain "pain" or punishments if the objectives are not met. Announcing goals to friends, colleagues and associates will strengthen commitment to achieving the goals and will provide the participant with ongoing support.

T is for Time.

Establish a time frame to achieve your desired outcomes. When you get specific with your goals, you will break them down into actions. Each action will have an associated schedule that triggers the clear and precise steps to be followed to complete each action. Get started as soon as possible.

The SMART system template encourages you to document a specific desired outcome that is measurable, achievable, relevant and timely, along with three actionable steps that are time sensitive and achievable.

Here are three ways to help you practice your SMART strategies:

1. Use the SMART template to establish a clear and concise strategy for your professional or private matters. It is easy to use, effective, and proven to deliver results.

2. Have fun and share the SMART template. Each time you can explain it to another person, your level of mastery increases. Master this tool to master your life.

3. Leverage the SMART template with associates at work. The more people in the workplace that use the template, the higher the awareness grows. The template stimulates action and ensures work tasks move along more quickly and more efficiently.

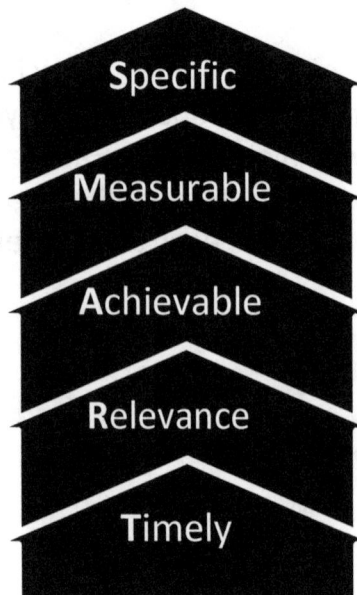

Specific

Measurable

Achievable

Relevance

Timely

A COACHING EXPERIENCE

A wonderful story is about a terrific woman called Kate. Kate was a former golf professional and she decided that she wanted to host her own sports radio program in Hong Kong. She came into our coaching sessions and she completely energized the environment.

Through the sessions, she utilized the SMART tool to gain precision, detail, and momentum in her quest.

S is for specific.
Kate knew she wanted a radio program.

M is for measurable.
Kate knew that she needed to meet at least three people a week in the media business. She first talked to her immediate contacts of around twenty-five people, expressing her dream to host a radio program. She then sought assistance from the associates in the class, around another twenty-five people. She was committed to mention to all her new contacts about her intention to host a radio program.

A is for Achievable.
Kate's attitude was world-class. She knew her specific and measurable approach was achievable. Her approach was filled with emotion, passion, and enthusiasm and everyone in our environment were encouraging and supportive of her drive and activities.

R is for relevant.
This is where she made it a MUST! Her break occurred when she was asked to help out with an event. Her clarity and

determination put her in a position where she got exposure to some decision-makers about radio in Hong Kong and when she was asked to "help out" with some radio work, she leapt at the opportunity.

T is for timing.

Kate set herself a six-month time frame to get a program. Her determination and ability to make it a 'must' got her a weekly program in less than ten weeks.

Kate's story illustrates that by employing the SMART tool you can achieve your goals!

Quality Questions - Measuring by being SMART

Rate yourself on a scale of 0 to 10, on how well your use of the SMART process in the workplace?

Rating _____

What three actions will improve your familiarity, confidence, and competence in using SMART in the office? Who and How, specifically can you use it with?

1) _____

2) _____

3) _____

Upon completion of these three actions, how will you feel and what rating would you give yourself in using the SMART process?

I will feel _____

Rating _____

*Be fully engaged in
the conversation you are having.
Listen actively and receive all the messages
your associate is telling you.*

ENTHUSIASTIC LISTENING

To take your coaching to the next level, you must develop an awesome impact coach's ear.

*Enthusiastic listening means you are fully
engaged in the conversation*

Shift your body, move your shoulders back, breathe deeply, smile and concentrate on the message being transmitted. By shifting your body you can get into a comfortable, receptive physiology to receive messages.

Listen to the nuances in the voice: the tone, the consistency, the timbre and the voice quality.

A coach is tuned in to pick up and notice emotions. You become accustomed to acknowledging and verifying them.

For example,
"You seem troubled or disturbed Daniel, would you like to share?"

Maintain eye contact. Empathize with the associate, because in doing so you convey your sincerity, interest and good intention.

Be patient, be focused and allow the speaker to finish their sentence or thought before you respond. Respond with questions and rephrase them at times to ensure that your interpretation of their message is clearly received and understood.

Be active in your listening. Probe with questions in a respectful, polite manner and remember to ask permission if you believe that your question may lead to some discomfort or misunderstanding.

"The greatest problem with communication is
we don't listen to understand.
We listen to reply.
When we listen with curiosity,
we don't listen with the intent to reply,
we listen for what's behind the words."
~ Roy T. Bennett

With these useful insights, the enthusiastic listener can make friends easily.

- Listen at least two times more than you speak. There is a reason why you have two ears and one mouth. Follow this rule and you are well on your way to being an awesome impact coach.

- Be alert. How would you sit if you were alert? How would you breathe to be alert? How would you feel if you were alert? Focus on being alert while you are proactively listening.

- Avoid one of the most frequently used rapport busting statements: "I know exactly how you feel." You can empathize, appreciate and respect but saying you know exactly how another human being feels is condescending and should be avoided.

Listen with curiosity.
Speak with honesty.
Act with integrity.

~ Roy T. Bennett

Quality Questions - Enthusiastic Listening

On a scale of 0 to 10, 0 being terrible and 10 being outstanding, how do you rate yourself as an enthusiastic listener in the workplace?

Rating _____

What three actions could you take in the next week to develop an awesome impact coach's ear for enthusiastic listening?

1) _____

2) _____

3) _____

If you were to accomplish the above tasks in the agreed upon time frame, what would your rating be for enthusiastic listening?

Rating _____

If your rating went up, terrific, or; if not, what would be one other step that you could do to be an "even better" enthusiastic listener?

_____

Ask awesome questions and you will

receive awesome answers

INTRODUCING AWESOME QUESTIONS

The quality of your life comes down to the quality of the questions that you ask yourself and others. An awesome question is brief, clear, focused, relevant and constructive. To increase the effectiveness of your questions, apply the word "specifically" to get your associates to give you brief, accurate, specific responses.

Asking quality questions is an essential skill for any coach to master in becoming an awesome impact coach.

Awesome questions are simple to remember
and simple to use
(5W's and 1H)
What, When, Where, Who, Why and How?

- To gain clarity ask, "What specifically, do you want?" followed by, "What do you truly want?"

- To discover the specific time frame, ask "When, specifically?"

- When you need an exact location, use "Where, specifically?"

- When you want to identify those involved, "Who, specifically?"

- When you want to develop a step by step plan, use "How, specifically?"

- Finally, the "Why, specifically?" question is extremely effective for tapping into pain and pleasure leverage areas, to spur positive and long-lasting behavioral change. You will learn more about leverage in the chapter 'On The Line - Leverage."

Here are three effective methods you can employ to improve the quality of your questions:

1. Be aware of questions that come into your head! Write them down. Focus and use positive, constructive and supportive questions like, "What can I learn from this experience?" or "Who can I thank today?" or "What am I grateful for?"

2. Avoid negative questions like "Why am I so stupid?" or "Why does this always happen to me?" or "What did I do

to deserve this?" All of these questions are answered by our subconscious mind in negative ways that fail to support, serve or contribute to a healthy, happy and prosperous life.

3. Ask quality questions in public, especially when you are in big groups of people. Asking questions will help develop your self-confidence and poise under pressure. It will also create positive attention directed towards you and contribute to the learning and knowledge of everyone in the room.

Asking quality questions is an essential skill for any coach to master in becoming an Awesome Impact Coach

Quality Questions - Introducing Awesome Questions

Asking better questions, on a scale of 0 to 10, 0 being terrible and 10 being outstanding, how do you rate your skill at asking quality questions?

Rating _____

What three actions could you take in the next month to develop your ability and skills at asking better questions?

1) _____

2) _____

3) _____

If you were to accomplish the above tasks in the next month, what would be your rating for asking quality questions?

Rating _____

If your rating went up, terrific, or; if not, what would be one other step that you could do to be "even better" at asking questions?

_____

On a scale of 0 to 10, 0 not committed and 10 absolutely committed, how committed are you at improving the quality of your questions?

Rating _____

Emotion leads to motion.
Energize your office with stimulating
activities for the mind, exercises for the body,
and empowerment for the soul!

MESMERIZE - ENERGIZE

In the movie "Field of Dreams" Kevin Costner was told to "build the field and people will come."

With blind faith, he built the ballpark and people did come from all around to watch his games. In the workplace, you can use a similar mantra. ***Build motivation and momentum, and the energy will flow.***

Energizing associates, team members and superiors is a process that requires commitment, persistence and dedication. Consistent, congruent and quality contributions made by the core energizing team will have positive long-term effects.

You can generate motivation and momentum within your teams in these ways:

- Motivate by establishing a tailor-made career plan that can benefit each employee and support long-term growth.

- Energize your associates through healthy and well-publicized employee recognition programs.

- Nurture the intellectual, personal and professional development of associates. Ensure that your associates participate in robust education and training programs throughout the year.

- Coordinate and sponsor opportunities to allow your associates to "make a difference" to society, the less fortunate and the environment. These activities will energize your office, and contribute to your community.

Increase the energy flow in your workplace by targeting these areas:

1. Social activities (bowling, picnics, dinner and dance) are excellent ways to get people to mingle, share and understand different sides of their associates.

2. Educational opportunities (in-house training, speaker's club, weekly talks, pot-luck lunches, yoga and wellness sessions) are some of the more popular activities to increase the energy flow in the office. You can even start a library or book sharing club in the office.

3. Acknowledgment of associates is a must for a company or organization that wants to retain and grow awesome staff. Organize regular recognition awards and publish a newsletter to share information about what's happening in the office. When your associates know they are appreciated, you will see awesome results.

Quality Questions - Mesmerize – Energize

On a scale of 0 to 10, 0 being terrible and 10 being outstanding, how do you rate yourself as a source of positive energy in the workplace?

Rating _____

What three actions could you take in the next month to contribute to the energy level in the workplace? What could you start, initiate or energize in your workplace?

1) _____

2) _____

3) _____

If you were to accomplish the above tasks in the next month, what would you rate yourself as an office energizer?

Rating _____

Time is your most valuable resource. Time is money, so make it a point to coordinate, organize, and invest it wisely.

PUNCTUALITY IS PROFESSIONAL

What is the greatest equalizer in life? With a world consisting of huge discrepancies and variations between wealth and poverty, what is the greatest equalizer in life that we all share?

If you answered by saying "time" then you are absolutely correct. Even the richest men in the world, Bill Gates and Warren Buffet, have only 24 hours in a day.

What makes them remarkable is their ability to process, review and prioritize reams of information and then still get things done, all within the same shared period of a single day.

How does it make you feel when someone is late for an appointment and makes you wait?

What thoughts go through your head when a person makes you wait? Do you start to question the person's sincerity, responsibility and ability?

These impressions do make a difference. If you get a reputation for being late, making people wait, or being absent-minded about time, it may negatively impact your professional life as well as your private life.

When developing peak performers, it is essential to coach them on the importance of time. With the permission of the associate, the awesome impact coach can work with them to shift their understanding of time and its values.

The coach should firstly understand the associate's existing mindset towards time. Using this information, the coach can help create a shift in the person's belief system by emphasizing the importance of punctuality and how it impacts on their career.

For example, you could ask,

"What will happen if you continue to be late?"

"If you don't improve your attendance, what will happen?"

These questions may create some discomfort for the associate, but can be a strong motivator to instigate a change in behavior.

Another great strategy is to tap into the associate's negative experiences of wasting time. Get them to share negative experiences related to waiting, as well as wasting other people's time.

Help them to view these situations as a waste of life's most precious commodity. Any or all of these methods can be used to alter, change and shift behavior patterns relating to time. These behavior shifts can be coached, tracked and measured if the associate truly desires to make the change.

An awesome impact coach can facilitate this shift and will work with associates to internalize the importance of respecting themselves and respecting other people's time.

Here are three key ways to master your schedule and punctuality:

1. Make journaling a habit to assist you to use your time more effectively, efficiently and productively.

2. Preview, prioritize and plan your week in advance. Prioritize key objectives for the week ahead and make sure you allocate more time to major tasks.

3. Allow for ample time to travel to meetings and appointments. If you are going to be late, advise the other party and apologize in advance. This extra effort will ensure that your counterpart feels respected and appreciated.

Quality Questions - Punctuality is Professional

Rate yourself on a scale of 0 to 10, on how well you allocate your most valuable asset, your time?

Rating _____

What three actions can you take in the next twenty-one days to become "even better" in planning or respecting time? Specifically, how can you invest your time "even more" wisely?

1) _____

2) _____

3) _____

Upon completion of these three actions, what rating would you give yourself for punctuality and time management?

Rating _____

Embrace a failure-proof mindset to create action and achieve results.
When your team views action as an opportunity to learn and grow, they will respond positively and continue to move forward, even when upsets happen.

ACTION ORIENTED

Coach your team to be confident, decisive and action-oriented.

Develop action plans with associates, include them in brainstorming sessions and use free flowing proactive questions such as;

"What steps do you feel that we should take?"
"How do you think we should handle this situation?"
"What resources will you require to get the results?"

In creating an action-oriented, coaching environment, you develop a proactive, supportive system that will nurture and bring out the best in your team.

In my first book, "The 6 Dimensions of Top Achievers" co-authored with Arthur Carmazzi, we dedicated an entire chapter to the development of the "failure-proof" mindset.

This concept focuses on creating a mindset of action, learning and growing. The failure-proof mindset works well for companies that want to shift from a blame culture to a coaching culture.

In a coaching culture, an awesome question to ask is "What did you learn from that experience?" When we have a failure-proof mindset, we respond positively and create congruency between the conscious and subconscious mind.

When you coach staff to be action-oriented you will gain these benefits:

- Clearer communication
- Greater mutual respect and understanding
- Improvements to working morale and initiative
- New possibilities to develop passions

While we all know that constructive and clear communication supported by fully developed action plans lead to improved results and higher success, it is not always followed. As Confucius stated, "To know and not to do is not yet to know".

How do we create an action-oriented, empowered and healthy workforce?

Here are three simple suggestions on what to avoid.

1. Avoid procrastination. Action is the antitoxin to a very dangerous corporate illness called procrastination. Coach an associate, draft a plan, share your ideas, persuade with confidence and TAKE Action!

2. Avoid blame culture syndrome. The peak performance coaching culture is the remedy for the blame culture syndrome. Nurture your associates and encourage coaching. Be supportive, collaborative and willing to learn!

3. Avoid perfectionist paralysis. The failure-proof system of think it, ink it, do it and review it, will banish the negative effects of perfectionist paralysis. Embrace failures and learn from them. Celebrate your failures and when you do fall, master the art of falling forward with every one of them. This will bring you ever closer to achieving your goal.

Quality Questions - Action Oriented – 1, 2, 3, GO!

Rate yourself for proactive action in the workplace, 0 is horrible, 10 is outstanding.

Rating _____

What three things can you do "even better" to nurture dynamic action and embrace the failure-proof mindset in the workplace?

1) _____

2) _____

3) _____

If you take these actions in the next ten days, what would your rating be?

Rating _____

If your rating has increased, terrific, or; if not, what additional action can you take to improve your learning and sharing in the workplace?

_____

*Nurture a caring approach.
Use clarity, attention, respect and energy to
help you become an awesome coach.*

CARING APPROACH

The impact coaching system is powered by a four-step mastery approach called CARE.

C is for clarity.

The care approach starts with the very clear and concise intention of assisting the associate to get clarity in understanding the problem, challenge or opportunity. In the ancient practice of word medicine, words were sacred. Remember words have power and a coach's effectiveness is amplified through the power of clarity.

A is for attention.

Attend to your associates. Be present with them and be acutely aware through using your three main senses of touch, sight, and sound. Heighten awareness by being alert. When you oxygenate your body by breathing deeply, stretching and moving, you will feel even more alert.

R is for respect

Respect your associates, respect yourself and respect the confidentiality of a coach/associate relationship. Be mindful that differences in perspectives, values, rules and beliefs do not necessarily make them "wrong." They are simply different. Judgment may cloud the coach's ability to provide constructive, clear and concise feedback and should be avoided within a coaching relationship.

E is for energy.

An awesome impact coach is aware of the powers of effective energy transfer. The coach is alert to the powers of clarity, awareness, respect, and the various energy frequencies. They can calibrate to the frequency of the associate and provide precise cues to facilitate breakthroughs, understandings and action plans.

The following steps will enable you to nurture the CARE in you:

1. Focus. Before your coaching session, relax your body, close your eyes and focus on your breathing. Take five or six deep breaths. Focus on being clear and making a difference.

2. Energize yourself. Move your arms, stretch and smile. By smiling you release endorphins that make you stronger, healthier and happier. This will put you in a more alert state and ready for Awesome Coaching.

3. Deliver value. Be completely present and experience coaching from many different perspectives. Play with the different roles that you regularly experience in day-to-day life. Ask the associate to imagine the current situation from another perspective. For example, as a CEO, what would you do in this situation? As a mother, what would you do in this situation? When the associate assumes this new role, they can tap into the resourceful states required for the role. When you step back and detach from the situation, problems begin to look different and opportunities suddenly materialize.

The skillset of an awesome impact coach is developed by utilizing the **CARE** approach. It is a foundation of coaching because it relies on the coach's sensitivity to calibrate all the energies and roles of the employees for the best results.

A COACHING EXPERIENCE

A great example of how the CARE approach can work happened within an ongoing "coaching project" being lived by my good friend, Dr. James Chia and his fourteen-year-old son, Daniel.

From September of 2004, James stopped giving pocket money to Daniel and they decided to come up with a project that would allow Daniel to gain some valuable insights into wealth and wealth creation.

James worked with Daniel to get clarity about his new project: to write a book of poems that could be sold to produce an income for Daniel.

At one level, James is directing Daniel and sharing with him the experience of turning his ideas into words, his words into a book, a book into a product and finally a product into money.

In the past when someone turned their thoughts into gold, they were called an Alchemist. I am pleased to share this story with you as it nurtures, inspires, and illustrates the Alchemist in all of us!

At another level of the project, James is sharing a project with his son and both of them are learning more about respect and the importance of relationships and teamwork.

The relationship dynamics involved in undertaking this project between Dan the Man and his father, Dr. James Chia, is truly a miracle-in-process. The miracle of communication, the miracle of cooperation, the miracle of change, and the miracle of completion!

The possibilities initiated by this idea, to get some pocket money, when powered by clarity, action, respect, and energy, is unlimited.

It underlines the realm of possibilities that are achievable when we employ the CARE Approach to communicate, coach, and work as a team.

Quality Questions - Caring Approach

Rate yourself as a practitioner of the CARE approach (clarity, attention, respect, and energy) in the workplace? How would your associates rate you?

Colleague Rating _____

Self Rating _____

What three things can you do "even better" to nurture the CARE skill set in the next fourteen days in the workplace?

1) _____

2) _____

3) _____

If you take these actions in the next fourteen days, what would your rating be?

Rating _____

Focus on your strengths.
Find and cultivate your skills,
gifts and abilities; develop a support team
around you and then nurture your personal
brand like a caring gardener.

TALENT MANAGEMENT

What would happen if you decided to focus on what you love doing? Would your results improve? Invest time in your talents and the quality of your results will soar.

Once a talent has been identified and a strategy of continuous improvement established, the talent requires some additional tools, techniques and strategies.

Talent management takes coaching to the next level by allocating additional time, focus and commitment to building, nurturing and developing a personal brand.

The Awesome Impact Coaching system approach to talent management emphasizes the individual and surrounds them with the best resources, as well as coaching in media, presentation skills, voice training, image design and personal branding.

In "The 6 Dimensions of Top Achievers," the vision dimension outlines ten key methods to attract visibility:
1.   Create a unique identity
2.   Create a different attitude
3.   Have a sense of authority
4.   Be a writer or presenter
5.   Create a press kit complementing your identity
6.   Learn to be an interesting storyteller
7.   Be willing to project real news
8.   Build rapport with others
9.   Learn excellent networking skills
10. Be a mentor, coach and a volunteer

To succeed in coaching a person in each of these areas takes discipline, commitment and a plan. Talent management for top-level managers, executives and business leaders may make use of specialized coaches for each area and should include a comprehensive strategy for consistent personal and professional branding.

By elevating any one of the keys to visibility, the other areas are magnified, and their personal earning potential and exposure increases exponentially.

Here are three bonus tips to becoming an awesome impact coach in talent management:

1. Develop your talent team. Have a resource base of awesome impact coaches with different areas of

expertise: Performance coach; Voice coach; Media coach; Technology coach; and World-class coaches from different disciplines. This will allow a talented individual to receive effective and efficient awesome impact coaching within the shortest possible time frame.

2. Invest your time. Be open with your ignorance. Increase your training, read, observe, and ask questions. Develop and get specialized coaching in areas where you can benefit from another person's expertise.

3. Be an advocate. Pay it forward with colleagues, associates and even competitors. Make it a habit to speak well of others, share business opportunities and become a raving fan of the people in your network. Being an advocate reflects well on you and others.

TALENT MANAGEMENT

Communication
Heritage   Style   Peer
                                 Group

Clothing &   Personal
Accessories   Tastes

Personal

Original   **Brand**   Location
Concept   & Habits

Body   Personal
Language   Unique   Transport
             Compliment
             Skill

Quality Questions - Talent Management

On a scale of 0 to 10, 0 being terrible and 10 being outstanding, how do you rate yourself as a developer of talent in your workplace?

Rating _____

What three actions could you take in the next month to add "even more" value to your colleagues and associates and to help them shine in their careers?

1) _____

2) _____

3) _____

If you were to accomplish the above tasks in the next month, how would you rate yourself as a talent manager?

Rating _____

Check your body posture, match and mirror, listen for language patterns, and be intently aware during your coaching sessions.

COACHING PHYSICALLY

Coaching eye to eye is an integral component of nurturing trust in a coaching relationship. The "Eye-to-Eye System" is the four-step methodology that accelerates the coach's ability to develop clearer communication at both a subconscious and conscious level.

Remember the eye-to-eye system

First, be aware that body posture does matter in coaching. Crossed arms, a tilt of the head, sitting forward, backwards, yawning; these are all communication hints that are picked up by the subconscious and conscious mind. The awesome impact coach is critically aware of the importance of body posture while coaching.

Second, employ the body posturing adjustment tools of matching or mirroring to develop clearer and more intuitive communication. A mirror movement is when the coach acts as a mirror. For example, if the associate lifts his left hand, the coach might move or shift their right hand.

The movement made by the coach is the mirror opposite of the movement made by the associate. The matching movement is when the coach makes the same movement.

Using the same example, the associate moves their right hand and so to match this movement the coach would move their right hand. This is not a tool to be used lightly. Mimicry and making fun of someone's movements is not the objective here. By using body posturing tools, the coach must have a sincere and respectful intention to build trust and connection with the associate.

Third, an awesome impact coach will look for patterns of language or keywords and phrases that the associate uses, and start to use them too. By utilizing keywords and shifting the tempo, speed, loudness or softness of their speech, the coach is able to move respectfully into the communication mode of the associate and develop a greater appreciation for their model of the world.

Fourth, look for differences with twice the awareness, listen for keywords with twice the attention, and even smell with twice the intensity.

Ask more questions and talk less

An awesome impact coach is aware, alert and able to shift his or her body posture to connect with the associate. By doing so, the coach can then lead the employee into an "even more" energized and resourceful state.

Here are three great ways to make your eye-to-eye coaching system more effective:

1. Review. Before approaching someone, conduct a quick review of the environment and the person's body posture. Use of primary senses: sight, sound, touch, smell and possibly even taste, to gauge the situation.

2. Be flexible. The more rules you have the less flexible you can be in using the body posturing eye to eye system.

3. Have fun with the eye to eye system. Practice it, use it and enjoy the learning process.

Quality Questions - Coaching Physically

On a scale of 0 to 10, 0 being terrible and 10 being outstanding, how do you rate yourself as an eye-to-eye coach?

Rating _____

What three actions could you take in the next week to develop your skills as an eye-to-eye coach?

1) _____

2) _____

3) _____

If you were to master the above tasks in the next week, what would your rating for eye-to-eye coaching be?

Rating _____

If your rating went up, terrific, or; if not, what would be one other step that you could do to be an "even better" eye-to-eye coach?

_____

Use your associate's fears and pleasures as positive and negative leverage, to create awesome change in their lives.

ON THE LINE - LEVERAGE

When will people change? What stops people from changing? Polls conducted at various impact coaching sessions throughout the Asia Pacific region, indicate that fear or the perception of fear or loss, is the number one reason why people avoid change.

Levers help to induce, drive, or empower change

The antidote for fear is action. By effectively employing appropriate quantities of pain, or perceived pain, and pleasure, or perceived pleasure, an awesome impact coach can effectively and eloquently steer associates toward their desired results.

As an awesome impact coach, one of the main objectives in working with or empowering an associate, is to help identify the key levers that can induce, drive or empower change. By understanding the levers of the individual, the coach can act as an agent of change.

Most human beings will do almost anything to avoid pain or perceived pain. If a coach knows about the associate's fears, such as a fear of loss or a fear of failure, the coach can ask questions that leverage on these fears to create certainty, motivation and inspiration towards the desired behaviors.

Alternatively, undesirable behaviors can be curtailed. In the same way, pleasure, or perceived pleasure, can also be utilized as a motivator or positive association for the associate and can help them to move towards the desired outcome.

For example, if an associate wishes to quit smoking, a coach may ask,

"Is there anything in your life that you love more than smoking?"

If they respond, "Yes, my children," the coach may then use the children as a change instrument to get the associate to change or alter their smoking behavior.

A possible change-inducing question could be,

"Do you want to see your children grow up?"

"Does smoking increase or decrease your chances of seeing the wedding of your child?"

For a positive association, the coach may ask a series of questions,

"How would it feel to be healthier?"

"Have you ever been healthier?"

"As a healthier person, would you be a smoker or a non-smoker?"

"And as a non-smoker, how would that make you feel and what would you look like?"

These questions can be utilized to tap into the experiences of the associate and can act as a magnet for new and empowering behavior.

Positive and negative associations such as pleasure and pain are key principles of peak performance coaching.

This is often referred to as positive and negative leverage: pleasure and pain, and reward and punishment. We use these associations daily, often subconsciously, to substantiate action or non-action. As a catalyst for change an awesome impact coach can utilize the principles of positive and negative leverage, pain and pleasure, as well as reward and punishment.

If you want to take your coaching to the next level, improve your competency in understanding the levers that make people change. These actions will improve your competency.

1. Ask permission. Some questions to gain leverage will result in sensitive answers, so get permission first before asking personal questions to get to the root of the matter. By asking their permission, the associate will often open up and be more receptive to starting the change process.

2. Be brave. Tough questions can make you feel uncomfortable. Take a deep breath, stay connected and remain grounded. Keep in mind where you want to go and what is the desired outcome of the coaching session.

3. Confirm and commit. A coach must get confirmation from the associate about the shift in reality that has occurred. Confirm the actions that are needed to continue the progress and get a commitment from the associate to implement one, two or three new actions as part of their change strategy.

Quality Questions - On the line – Leverage

On a scale of 0 to 10, 0 being terrible and 10 being outstanding, how do you rate yourself at finding the key leverage point(s) of change for your coaching clients?

Rating _____

What three actions could you take in the next month to develop "even greater" expertise at identifying the key levers of change in your coaching clients?

1) _____

2) _____

3) _____

If you were to focus on identifying key levers of change and accomplish the above tasks in the next month, how would you rate yourself at finding key levers?

Rating _____

If your rating went up, terrific, if not, what would be one other step you could do, to be "even better" at finding levers of change?

_____

On a scale of one to ten, how committed are you to master the skills of leverage as a vehicle to make a difference in people's lives?

Rating _____

See the world through New Eyes.
Notice the flowers, the birds,
your friends and your family.

ALERTNESS – NEW EYES

In his bestseller, "The Power of Now," Eckert Tolle shares the importance of staying in the present. He encourages us to let go of the past, not to worry about the future, and instead to focus on the present, the now, the moment. This is the foundation for being alert.

Smile and display some appreciation for all
the beauty around you

As an awesome impact coach, we are always looking for great models, techniques or tools to add to our repertoire of transformation. One of my favorite models to learn about Alertness is using memories of when my son, Justin, was four years old.

A four-year-old child is remarkably alert. Alert for a four-year-old is all about being fully engaged. Children are remarkable because they are goal-oriented, focused, action driven, flexible and most often very successful in their quest.

Watch a four-year-old around an ice cream parlor. They are goal oriented.

thought - I want some ice cream

They focus.

thought - how can I get some ice cream

They take action.

ask - "May I have an ice cream please?"

They are flexible.

if you say yes, great;
if you say no, they start wailing

Either way, the outcome is often successful.

They get the ice cream

As an impact coach, we have a lot to learn from children, and it all starts with their eyes.

Children see things through a term I like to call, "New Eyes". As a coach, when you start to see things through new eyes it will begin to transform you and your coaching.

Coaching through "New Eyes" is tapping into a higher sense of alertness. It is coaching with a new feeling of enthusiasm, a spirit of curiosity and an appreciation of the new (and all things are new!).

Here are three fantastic strategies to bring "new eyes" into your coaching.

1. Physiology First. Move your body and get into a state of anticipation. Can you remember being a four-year-old child at a birthday party? Get prepared physically and mentally. Look forward to something that's very exciting for you!

2. Be a Child. Be curious, honest and in the moment. Be interested, learn and develop. Play like a child. Engage fully. Focus on taking something apart. Being childlike is very different from being childish.

3. Be Alert. Be aware and ask, ask, ask and remember to listen and learn. Be externally focused. Respectfully and tactfully work to achieve what you are focused on.

Quality Questions - Alertness - New Eyes

Rate yourself as a practitioner of seeing with "new eyes", especially in the workplace. How would your colleagues rate you?

Colleague Rating _____

Self Rating _____

What three things can you do "even better" to be aware of the powers of now and seeing with "new eyes" in the next fourteen days?

1) _____

2) _____

3) _____

If you take these actions in the next fourteen days, what would your rating be?

Rating _____

Kick start your creativity by asking yourself "what would my role model do when faced with this situation?"

CREATIVE SOLUTIONS

If you have ever had difficulties convincing your employees, getting a consensus, or getting people to buy into your agenda, it may be because your staff did not feel part of the process.

The coaching process has to be interactive. If you do not engage associates in the process, you will come up with your plan, but it will not be their plan. You must develop a creative approach to include others.

Be outrageous and remember to have a failure proof mindset

Use these ideas to spark creativity:

- Define the opportunity, desired state or preferred outcome. A problem is a challenge and a challenge is an opportunity.

- Activate creative alternatives and be outrageous with some of the possible solutions. If you have a blockage when it comes to being creative, perhaps you could use a creative person like Walt Disney or Steven Spielberg as a model. Ask yourself what Walt Disney would do, say, or feel in this situation. Or what actions Steven Spielberg would take. The answers to these modeling questions will unleash the unlimited world of possibilities and dramatically increase creative alternatives!

- Engage associates to come up with specific action steps. Coach your colleagues and get them to put their suggestions, ideas and recommendations into a SMART format.

- Confirm an understanding. Repeat the actionable steps, measure the level of certainty and adopt new actions until the associate has a high level of confidence and certainty of success. Get reassurance and commitment from associates to take action, by asking them what level of certainty they have that they will take action, and then get them to verbalize their commitment.

- Plan the follow-up and the next session, and leave associates in a positive, confident state. Ask them how they would feel if they had already completed the tasks. By asking them this question, we increase the probability of success because the brain does not distinguish between perceived success and actual success. This form of visualization allows associates to have the positive experience prior to physically experiencing it, thereby increasing their conviction that they will be successful.

Developing creativity is a free and open area of study leading to amazing developments as a coach. Here are three more ways to enhance creativity:

1. Think out of the box. A coach can ask specific questions to get associates to think using a new reality, or with a new pattern of behavior. Some coaches like to ask the person to "throw away the box." Play with the words and the terminology!

2. Be outrageous. Yes, Walt Disney was outrageous – an amusement park in the middle of an orange grove – how outrageous! Coaching can create outstanding and often outrageous results.

3. Play with Polarities. Big, small, hate, love, white, black- using polar differences can be an effective breakthrough tool for coaching. An awesome impact coach's greatest strength is often providing a mirror for associates to see themselves. By exploring the polar opposite to what is the main area of focus, impact coaching can lead to dramatic shifts in perspective and amazing creative alternatives.

A COACHING EXPERIENCE

One of my clients, a junior executive for an international bank, had a favorite saying whenever colleagues, friends and family confronted her. She used to say, **"I don't care,"** at least ten times a day.

During our first coaching session, she must have said it five times in the first ten minutes. I noticed the "language pattern" immediately and decided to interrupt her pattern by starting to use the same language pattern.

I then asked her if she liked people using that phraseology with her. She smiled and said, "I don't care!"

I told her that this was a good example of polarities. "What?" she asked. Rather than answer her directly I asked her if perhaps the reason she uses the phrase, "I don't care" so often, is that she really does care. I said, "In fact, I think that you do care very much."

She smiled when I said this and shared with me that she does care a lot, perhaps even too much. She reflected and said that she started using that phrase when she was young and her parents divorced. It made her feel strong, in control, and not affected by the outside world.

I told her that unfortunately it sounded phony and that the phrase "I don't care" hid her true caring, loving, and supportive nature.

I asked her,

"Do you want to be remembered as someone who does care or someone who does not care about people?"

She smiled and replied, "Someone who cares." She decided that day to stop using that phrase and to replace it with "I do care," because that is how she wants people to remember her.

Today she is a caregiver and an awesome coach and I now think of her as a person whose real strength is her ability to care unconditionally.

Changing that single language pattern, and in turn shifting from one extreme to the other, allowed her to take control of her communication and change her life!

Quality Questions - Creative Solutions

On a scale of 0 to 10, 0 being terrible and 10 being outstanding, how do you rate yourself as a creative solutions provider in the workplace?

Self Rating _____

What three actions could you take in the next week to develop your skills as a creative solutions provider in the workplace?

1) _____

2) _____

3) _____

If you were to master the above tasks in the next week, what would your rating for creativity be?

Rating _____

If your rating went up, terrific, or; if not, what would be one other step that you could do to be "even more" creative?

_____

Everyone deserves sincere and timely feedback. Be honest, supportive and helpful to create even better performance.

HARMONIOUS FEEDBACK

How does it make you feel when you get feedback from someone significant in your life? Can you imagine getting feedback from someone significant just once a year?

Yet, year after year, most associates are rated and judged by their superiors just once. Associates receive little or no feedback on how they are performing on a daily, weekly, monthly, or even quarterly basis.

In the coaching environment, everyone is encouraged to utilize the tools, techniques and processes of impact coaching to enhance the feedback loop, regularly and consistently.

Feedback can be harmonious and lead to better performance. Unfortunately, some feedback can also lead to disharmony, and can even lead to ill feelings or a communication breakdown.

Handled with honesty, sincerity and integrity, feedback will often lead to greater awareness and understanding of the associate's communication patterns. Applied regularly, consistently and proactively, top-down feedback can be turned into a 360-degree feedback process that includes reassessment, re-strategizing and, most importantly, achieve desired results.

An advanced module in the impact coaching system also utilizes a 360-degree feedback loop wherein feedback can include input from subordinates, superiors and other associates. This system allows the associate to realize the varied messages that are being delivered to different colleagues at different levels. The feedback received from this model is an excellent platform for coaching and leadership development programs.

Feedback is an essential tool for improving the performance of an individual or a team. Three key principles in providing feedback are,

1. Celebrate variety. Different people have different areas of expertise. Recognize and celebrate the success of your colleagues.

2. Ask for permission to give feedback. When you ask permission, it is usually appreciated. Give feedback

with sincerity, respect and integrity.

3. Give feedback regularly. Make it a habit to give people sincere praise and feedback. Develop a mindset of showing appreciation and gratitude. It will amaze you how easy it is to be genuine and sincere in your relationships.

A COACHING EXPERIENCE

In one recent coaching engagement, a fifty-year-old mother named Mary was troubled by her relationship with her twenty-four-year-old daughter, Sara. Coaching Mary was always a treat as she was mature, loving, and caring, but I could see that this issue was causing her considerable stress.

Mary wanted to develop her relationship with Sara but would say things that triggered anger, hostility and hurt in Sara.

In giving feedback to Mary, I was able to highlight her communication with Sara. Specifically, Sara had noted that her mom, "always told her what to do".

My strategic feedback question to Mary was,

"How would you feel if someone always told you what to do?"

Mary sat stunned for a moment! I then asked,

"If you continue to talk AT your daughter like that, what will happen to your relationship?"

As a tear started to well in Mary's eye, I quickly seized the opportunity to gain further leverage and asked,

*"Can you imagine your relationship with your daughter in five years if you continue to talk AT her?
Will there be a relationship?
Does this matter to you?"*

The tears started to flow as Mary began to visualize the future she was creating through her communication. I let her continue to cry for a moment before I asked my next question.

"Are you now willing to change your pattern of communication with your daughter?"

She nodded. "So what do you need to do?" Mary smiled and quickly responded, "Ask more questions."

I smiled and encouraged her to do so. She smiled back at me, took a deep breath, and with a new air of confidence stated, "I need to ask my daughter questions, show interest in her life, and hold back on the advice."

I nodded and asked Mary,

"How committed are you to making this happen in the next seven days, on a scale from one to ten?"

She smiled and said "10!"

Quality Questions - Harmonious Feedback

On a scale of 0 to 10, 0 being terrible and 10 being outstanding, how do you rate your ability to offer sincere constructive feedback to associates in the workplace? How about in your homelife?

Work Rating _____

Home Rating _____

What three actions could you take in the next month to enhance your expertise in sharing sincere constructive feedback in your personal or professional life?

1) _____

2) _____

3) _____

If you were to master the above tasks in the next month, what would your rating for sharing sincere constructive feedback be?

Rating _____

If your rating went up, terrific, or; if not, what would be one other step that you could do to be "even better" at providing sincere harmonious feedback?

_____

On a scale of one to ten, how committed are you to master the skills of providing sincere harmonious feedback as a vehicle to make a difference in people's lives?

Rating _____

The Last Word - Epilogue

Thank you for investing the time, energy and curiosity in reading this book.

If you have reached the epilogue, I would like to congratulate you and thank you for your commitment to excellence and perseverance in completing this journey.

Ancient Chinese script suggests that a journey of a thousand miles starts with a single step and I am hopeful that your journey may be enhanced by a word, thought, or process that has been shared in Get 2020 Vision - Awesome Coaching.

When we first set out to update the Get 2020 Vision Edition of Awesome Coaching, my editor and friend Tracey Regan encouraged me to update the book and to share on new topics that I found inspiring, scary or relevant to life in 2020 and beyond.

As I was transitioning through some monumental changes in my life, I elected to focus on mental wellness and to further explore effective strategies I have found to be helpful, not only to myself but to a large number of my coaching clients.

Big changes in life have the biggest effect on our mental wellness. For me, moving to Canada choosing to be a caregiver for my elderly parents after over 30 years living in Asia, while going through a divorce and career changes, left me facing some significant physical and mental challenges.

I must admit when I first started writing this book, I certainly didn't imagine what would unfold, be created and evolve from the experience of collaborating, connecting and co-creating the Get 2020 Vision Edition of Awesome Coaching.

As I reflect on the past twelve months, I invite the metaphor of healthy, wealthy and wise as headline topics.

HEALTHY

MENTAL WELLNESS

My journey with mental illness and mental wellness has evolved over the years, as it does for many, and continues to offer great insights and observations. This year, I placed my thoughts down on paper and chose to re-design this book around the theme of mental health.

In my studies of Epigenetics, I have been influenced by Dr. Bruce Lipton and Dr. Joe Dispenza, as well as the past decade of conversations, discourses and altered states of consciousness work with Dr. George Bien and Dr. George Blair West. With the assistance of both Dr. Georges', I was able to trace mental illness deep into my genetic code.

I believe trauma, scars, doubt and pain are transmitted from generation to generation, both genetically and experientially through genetics, nurture and nature. I was raised in a family that loved yet they were often triggered by traumas from the past, and this is a common trait in most of our lives.

My father had family members who suffered from schizophrenia, while his father suffered PTSD following World War 2. My mother's family experienced poverty, sexual and physical abuse, and fled China as refugees for a better life in Canada. All of these experiences have an impact on future generations, as it did mine.

My approach to health is greatly influenced by my interest in Eastern medicine. I have studied to instructor, practitioner and senior practitioner level, courses in Meditation, Yoga, Chinese CHI, Japanese KI energy work, massage, Chinese and Indian tantric healing, Indian Ayurvedic, Hypnotherapy, and Shamanic Healing, as well as modalities in Family Constellation, Neuro-Linguistic Programming, Time Line Therapy, and altered state of consciousness processes.

I am incredibly grateful for my family, friends and associates who are professionals in the healthcare systems across the Western world. While we do not always agree on specific topics, they have taught me the importance of nutrition, restful sleep and the intermittent use of prescribed medicine, as well as the Western protocol in dealing with illness, disease and pain.

The perspective and approach they bring to care-giving, patient care and navigating the healthcare system in Canada, has assisted me to embrace the best of Eastern and Western approaches.

Below, I have detailed my recipe for mental wellness, and I invite you to tailor and adapt my strategy into an evolving plan for you that may optimize your mental health.

1. Daily exercise, movement or stretching.

2. Prayer or meditation for 1 minute or 11 minutes or 111 minutes, daily or three times a week.

3. Eat healthy nutritious nurturing foods that elevate your energy and vibration. Salads, fresh fruit and 'live' foods are optimal for most people. It is always valuable to monitor your food and start to write down your food intake.

4. Drink healthy clean water. Eight glasses are recommended and reduce drinks containing sugar and carbonated products.

5. Laugh and bring more laughter into your life. Laughter releases natural endorphins and dopamine which contribute to healthy digestion and physical homeostasis.

6. Natural sunlight will contribute to your wellness by triggering vitamin D and the secretion of Oxytocin which helps with mental and physical well being.

7. Express kindness, forgiveness and generosity. Start your gratitude journal and write kind and nice messages to yourself and others. This will assist with serotonin levels which bring optimism and positivity into your mental and physical well being.

I was inspired to put this plan into action again recently when I was diagnosed with a high probability of prostate cancer. My initial reaction was disbelief and I began by questioning the system and the testing methodology. I found the testing to be inaccurate and was inspired to get into better shape, as my follow-up examination was scheduled for six weeks after the original tests.

I started eating salads, drank ten glasses or more of water, reduced my rice and bread intake, and started walking at least 15,000 to 25,000 steps per day. I also meditated, prayed and performed yoga daily. My prayers were for health and wellness and I decided to infuse laughter, giggles and humorous perspectives into my daily activities and conversations. My key empowering question was, "What is funny about this or where is the humor in this experience?"

My healthy strategies worked, and on my follow-up test my PSA levels dropped from 37 to 2.3, I had lost about 7.4kg and I was healthier, happier and ever more grateful than I had been for the past ten years. I even focused on immense gratitude to the doctor who misdiagnosed, as the diagnosis had inspired me to make positive changes to my everyday life.

A big part of the inspiration to write this Mental Wellness Edition of Awesome Coaching is in honoring the health care practitioners, such as my sister, who have taught me directly and indirectly through their commitment to wellness, healthcare and service. One such health care professional who I admire for her incredible courage, belief and action, is New Zealand based International Red Cross senior nurse, and Florence Nightingale Award Winner, Gurudev Singh.

GD, as she is affectionately known, has served in some of the most challenging, difficult and chaotic environments across the globe. She has volunteered in dangerous hot spots including Iraq during the war, the Ebola outbreak in Africa, assisting refugees in Asia and relief work wherever the International Red Cross requires health care professionals to serve humanity.

GD has taught me that 'practice makes progress,' and that communication and 'speaking one's truth' is key to building trust and a pathway to sleeping well and doing a professional job. I am incredibly grateful to have a dear friend like GD who has given me perspective on mental, physical and healthcare issues in some of the most extreme situations that humanity faces.

SACRED LIFE

Imagine awakening from a peaceful slumber at 5:15 am by a frantic parent as her beloved spouse of over fifty years has fallen and is howling in pain on the floor. March 16th was the day, the day before my mother's 80th birthday, and I was jettisoned into the role of caregiver as per the identity I have curiously undertaken since returning to Canada.

For the next ninety minutes, I explored ways to get my father out of pain and into a peaceful position. Fortunately, we were able to add comfort to his positioning on the floor yet each time we attempted to move him, he hollered with agony and insisted that I leave him.

In hindsight, when someone is in that level of pain, I would recommend calling in the professionals immediately, but as my father insisted on 'being left on the floor,' I relented, moved to acceptance and retreated to my room. An hour later, my mother called me to assist my father to the toilet. We were able to move him into the bathroom, but not without him experiencing extreme pain and twice he whispered, "Leave me alone to die." I found my thoughts wavering from cynical to compassionate, from provoking to a patient caregiver. It's amazing the polarities we face in critical situations.

After calling my sister, a healthcare professional, her advice was direct and clear. "Call a paramedic, get him checked out and do it now." My mother insisted on some agreement from my father which would not come for another five hours. She finally called the paramedics 12 hours after the fall at 5pm. The paramedics did a wonderful job and entering the emergency department we were greeted by a full staff of health care professionals outfitted in anti-pandemic overalls, face masks and gloves. We were restricted to one visitor per patient, so I took my leave and headed out to pick up my son Justin, as he was visiting Brampton to celebrate his grandmother's 80th birthday.

So to recap – My father has a fractured femur and is admitted to hospital during the COVID-19 pandemic, which is most severe for senior citizens. One of my best friends has recently committed suicide. My marriage has collapsed and I am diagnosed with a high probability of prostate cancer. I am unemployed in a fast-changing world, and my investments have taken a hit in the global financial meltdown due to the effects of the pandemic. I have what is known as a cluster of transitioning events that could easily lead to major depression.

Now I'm not telling you all this for compassion or empathy. I am highlighting what a cluster of events looks like, and would like to bring your awareness to the fact that many millions of people across the world, could be going through a similar cluster, brought on by the COVID-19 pandemic.

All of us need to be observant, not only of our own thoughts, but to be aware of what others may be going through. At this time, it is more important than ever to share strategies that will enable us to be more resilient and strengthen our mental wellness.

In my recent role as caregiver to my elderly parents, I am reminded that the elderly are not only at a higher risk from COVID-19, but also at high risk of mental illness. From our chats over tea discussing elderly care globally, I am grateful for the fraction of wisdom I have learned from my mentor and teacher, Gillie Robinson. As the author of many of New Zealand's elderly care protocols and procedures, Gillie has taught me how self-care is paramount to being an effective caregiver.

Gillie embraces this essential element with a keen mind and perspective to systemize, explore best practices, implement robust procedures and ultimately be responsible for her watch. Whether learning directly from her, her books or her research, I truly appreciate her contribution and service to the health care profession, and her insights into the care of the elderly.

WEALTHY

FINANCIAL UNCERTAINTY

Financially, with the COVID-19 pandemic spreading around the world and wreaking havoc on financial markets since December 2019, people are facing devastating declines in their stock portfolios and retirement funds. Many retirement funds have been decimated, with the elderly most at risk. Trillions of dollars of global wealth have been wiped out and many of my friends and family who have been saving for their retirement, are shell-shocked from the experience.

Working in the financial markets for much of my life, I have weathered the storm of three major financial crashes. As a risk manager in Japan during the 1987 market crash, I observed the Japanese market fall from 39k to 7k. During the September 11, 2001 crash, I was working as a bond trader managing a billion-dollar portfolio. And as an entrepreneur during the 2008 Global Financial Crisis, we closed nine businesses operating in four countries. These life experiences have equipped me with a level of optimism and calm when engaging in today's uncertainty, and I have a respectful acceptance of the financial markets.

I must admit if this happened thirty years ago, I may have panicked. It would have likely kept me up at night, and at that time, I would have seriously considered ending my life. With the approaches that I have shared in this book and the research that was part of presenting this book, I have chosen to be proactive, positive and present to my feelings, my fears, and my focus.

If you are facing financial stress, or suffering financial hardship due to COVID-19, I invite to you focus on positivity, focus on humor and on what you can do today, in this moment, to nurture wellness, be healthy and to stay positive.

As I share this approach, some of you might say "it's hard," or "it's easier to say than to do." Respectfully, I smile and invite you to re-read the chapter on the power of words, (Page 145) or reframe your beliefs and shift your focus. I truly believe change can be "smooth and simple," or it can "be hard." In fact, it can be what you choose it to be.

As the pandemic spreads throughout the world and fear is being rallied on social media, by our governments and by the international news community, it is up to you should you choose to be resourceful and explore areas that you can influence, such as, your mental wellness, your positive focus and actions that contribute to you feeling resourceful. Change your words, shift your beliefs and infuse positive action and activities into your daily rituals and habits and you will move forward with positivity and an active approach that will serve you, your family and your community.

CELEBRATING LIFE BY HONORING DEATH
Since my return to Canada, I have experienced the death of two aunts, one cousin and my mother's family pet.

The passing of my aunt Helen was beautiful as our family had an opportunity to connect, support and communicate with love and light about the life and times of my mother's sister.

The conversations were healing, kind and compassionate. I was able to connect with my cousin, previously known as my 'fighting cousin' from our childhood battles in the park and disputes over food, habits and opinions. We were able to express kindness, appreciation and gratitude that would have made her mother proud and happy to see the family so peaceful, respectful and joyful in honoring her life, and her legacy.

You might ask, "How did you do it? How did you and your cousin let go of all the past anger, upset or pain?" Fortunately, my cousin and I both had a willingness to communicate, share and listen with respect and curiosity. We both felt blessed, we were willing to learn and forgive. There was an invitation to heal and we invited healing miracles into our relationship. We invited her mother, my aunt, to be involved in the process and I had the feeling that my Aunt Helen was watching from above and smiling with joy and appreciation that we loved her enough to let go of our decade-old disputes.

This experience was very different from the passing of my cousin. My cousin's passing from drowning was kept quiet from the family and the pain and sadness were expressed via social media. I reached out to connect to my cousin's family and while we did not have any follow through on either side, it did teach me to accept the choices and wishes of others, and that a simple prayer or kind wish for others does lead to an amazing healthy mindset.

Finally, there was the passing of my mother's dog, my little brother Cody.

It was tragic, sad and gut-wrenching as my mother decided to put her finest, cutest and most beloved dear doggie down. As Cody's health deteriorated, my mother decided quickly and swiftly to put Cody down to minimize his pain and suffering. The decision was painful for my mother, yet it was her way of honoring and loving her beloved pet and much-loved family member. While my mother still misses Cody, we do appreciate him immensely and we have fond memories of his joy, uniqueness and quirkiness.

Death is a fascinating topic to discuss and I invite you to explore and express with your friends and family. We can all have different views of life and death and with respect, I would like to share some of my perspectives and I hope they may assist you on your life journey.

I believe that life is special and that our time on this planet is finite. I love honoring the moment, respecting the universe and living life with appreciation, gratitude, love and kindness.

I respect death and find that welcoming death, honoring memories and truly living life brings calm, peace and harmony into my being.

I am grateful to Death and that it shines brightly in my life. Death has taught me an immense amount on how to savor life, appreciate life and live life to the fullest.

When I left Canada in 1986, I had a knowingness that each time I returned for a short visit, when I left it may be the last time that I saw my parents. I chose to embrace this belief as it allowed me to tell them how much I loved them, how much I appreciated them and how much I value our time together.

Once I started this tradition, I noticed that the number of arguments, disagreements and disputes greatly declined and that very little time was spent sweating over the small stuff and that most of our time was focused on honoring, celebrating and cherishing magical moments. As the years passed, I shifted the word magical to miraculous moments.

Yes, I believe in miracles and Yes I believe that you are a miracle.

My journey with death and awareness around the circle of life grew tenfold during my time in Singapore and my close friendship with palliative care professional and hospice caregiver, Nurse Peppa. She taught me about compassion and professionalism, as well as respecting service in the face of death.

Peppa shared stories of expressing compassion by listening to people's last wishes, painting fingernails or styling hair of dying teens; she would arrange last meals or special deserts for dying seniors.

Nicknamed Death Nurse, our conversations were often animated, often profoundly deep, and sometimes morbid, yet always we spoke with truth, compassion and care. I acknowledge and truly honor the care of the hospice workers, palliative care professionals and caregivers. Over the years, I have met many caring people, yet my experience with Death Nurse has taught me so much about life by celebrating and respecting death.

WISE

LIFE OF MIRACLES
Since I welcomed the word miracles into my life, my vocabulary and my consciousness, I have noticed that miracles materialize or show up in my life.

I love miracles and my left brain likes the fact that statistically, we are all miracles.

Meeting a stranger, having an amazing conversation, and appreciating them as if they are my soul mate or soul cluster partner or twin flame, is an honoring that has allowed me to transform one-off conversations into life-changing moments.

What you take away from this book or how you apply it, or what little word, phrase or process might ring to you or your spirit, is a miracle to me. I invite you to explore, embrace or express miracles in your life and I hope you can feel like the miracle that you are. May miracles shine bright in your life.

My intention is that this book can serve you on your journey. It is my prayer that a story, poem or an invitation can bring richness to your life.

It is my hallucination that a challenge, an exercise or a statistic might trigger an awakening. May curiosity or an interest to explore, challenge or incite you to engage your mind, body or spirit with enthusiasm, or anger, or love and that your life becomes a little bit brighter.

May love, light and laughter guide or redirect your next steps or miracles on your journey.

I invite the Awesomeness in you to shine brightly. I invite some awe to shine brightly in your life.

Moreover, I thank the awesome people, like you, who have inspired my growth, my life and my legacy.

Get 2020 Vision - Awesome Coaching is an invitation to evolve.

To evolve with excitement
To evolve with vitality
To evolve with optimism
To evolve with love
To evolve with vision
To evolve with enthusiasm

Congratulations on bringing Get 2020 Vision to completion.

May we EVOLVE with kindness, compassion, love and light. Namaste.

Dave is passionate about enabling the growth in others.

What he learns, he aims to share through compassionate guidance and wisdom, such that the communities around him can express themselves in truly meaningful ways.

A father figure worth sharing!
- Justin Rogers

Though it may be hard to see the light,

In times of freeze, fight or flight,

Know that there is a purpose for each pain,

Compassion allows your soul to grow and gain,

Beyond each point, you will never be the same.

Wendy Kwek

A Wish For You

I wish you sunshine and flowers, joy and happiness,
A love that lasts forever; laughter and success.
But life's not always like that, and even if it was,
Would we still wonder?
Would we still cry?
Would the grass be greener on the otherside?
A life well-lived has ups and downs,
Mistakes, hard times and plenty of frowns.
But lessons learned and strength is grown,
When the unexpected comes to tip our throne.
So value each moment; one at a time,
Don't worry too much; enjoy the climb.
Take the good with the bad, make the most of each day,
And life will unfold in a natural way.
I wish you all that life may bring; the easy and the
hard,
And know your life will be amazing, though perhaps a
little scarred.

Tracey Regan

tracey regan
All Things Writing!

With Thanks!

Mary Rogers, Nurse Kim, Lee Anne, Ellen, Elena, Goddess of Light, Natanya, Sueanne, Anna, Ms Jolly, Tahira, Supermum, Karen, Elaine, Carol, Barbara, Amanda, Joanne, Mette, Masami, Tamami, Grace, Yuka, Tara, Cathy, Carolyn, Francis, Deb, Debbie, Tracey, Angie, Angela, Cany, Gillie, Rebecca, Dina, Dianne, Tini, Gloria, Getrude, GD, Maya, Melinda, Anne, Sue, Susan, Sara, Victoria, Wendy, Yvette, Yvonne, Zara, Yolanda, Pamela, Patricia, Penelope, Maria, Mother Mary, Gaia, Gail, Rachelle, Rochelle, Gwen, Harri, Michelle, Marilyn, Betty, Berni, Aroha, Shazar, Sahaja, Cindy, Cynthia, Suzanne, Cecilia, Pia.

Book cover designed by Lorenza Minghetti

Lorenza is a freelance graphic designer and visual communicator based in Perth, Western Australia. She helps businesses communicate with their existing and potential clients with beautiful, clean and functional designs. Lorenza provides design solutions that will reach your target audience and communicate your key messages.

For more information please visit www.lorenzaminghetti.com or email lorenza@lorenzaminghetti.com